# THE BLESSING OF THE CELTIC CURSE

## THE SAINTS OF SAVANNAH

LEIGH EBBERWEIN

Old Fort Press
Savannah, Georgia

The Blessing of the Celtic Curse



Old Fort Press
Savannah, Georgia

ISBN: 978-1-7376152-1-7 (Paperback)

ISBN: 978-1-7376152-0-0 (E-book)

Cover design: Okay Creations



❀ Created with Vellum

# WE MUST TALK

SAVANNAH, GEORGIA

The Cathedral bells tolled at the exact moment Kathleen stepped out through the church's massive mahogany doors. She had been in the same spot hundreds of times before, but that morning felt different, and she couldn't pinpoint why. The chill in the air blew against her face, causing her eyes to sting for a split second. She slowly drew in a breath of air and was startled when she exhaled with a sigh. All of her senses were alive, and she felt a stirring deep in her soul. She did a quick scan of her surroundings, expecting to find something out of place, but was met only with the comforting embrace of her home: Savannah.

A smile briefly flickered across her face as she scuttled down the church's granite stairs towards home. Dodging the glances from tourists on a passing trolley, she crisscrossed Lafayette Square and walked along the red brick sidewalk on

Abercorn Street. A week had passed since Easter, and all of Savannah was blossoming. The downtown squares were filled with azaleas, daylilies, tulips, and daffodil blooms against a backdrop of Confederate jasmine. On spring mornings, a yellow layer of pollen covered everything. The local television weatherman often warned viewers about the high pollen count. But that day, the weather was perfect: crisp and clear. Still, something felt different.

Most mornings, she would take the long route home around Forsyth Park. She always tried to squeeze 30 minutes of walking into her daily schedule to offset years of eating good ole Southern cooking, but that morning Clary's Restaurant was calling her name, and she knew their food would ease her troubles. They had the best breakfast in Savannah and were right around the corner from her home on Jones Street. The aroma of bacon wafting down Abercorn Street grew stronger and stronger, and just like an old dog with its nose in the air, the smell began to guide her feet towards the cafe. The temptation was too overwhelming, so she postponed her walking time until that afternoon.

She strolled into Clary's, said hello to the cashier and the regular customers, and sat at the long counter. She always felt odd sitting alone, watching all the busy people planning their days. But at the counter, she was safe. Seriously, who was she kidding? She loved the counter. She peeked in the large mirror behind the bar to survey the room, and got caught by a little boy who matched her stare. As if on cue, he stuck his tongue out at her so she scrunched her face and crossed her eyes in reply. When he laughed, his parents finally looked up from their cell phones and she turned her attention to the menu.

After drinking so much coffee that she was sloshing,

Kathleen began her short walk home. As she approached the house, she dug in her purse for the keys and glanced through the glass panels of the front door. Their dachshund Beau – short for General Beauregard – was wagging his tail but waiting patiently, in his non-judgmental way. She calmly talked to him through the glass, praying his tiny dachshund bladder could withhold his happiness.

Walking inside, she began her morning routine: feed animals, water plants, and open all of the street side blinds. With her chores finished, she sat quietly at her desk and heard the parlor door creak. She looked up just in time to recognize the faint glow of what she referred to as the Pink Lady floating down the hall and disappearing into the kitchen. When she was younger, she tried desperately to figure out why the ghost popped in and out of her life. But after 25 years, she accepted the fact that she would never have answers. There were just quick glimpses that over time became a welcome sight.

They certainly weren't the only house haunted in Savannah. Local tourist companies capitalized on paranormal entertainment at several of Savannah's old houses. It was not uncommon to see the infamous convertible hearse full of tourists, toddies in hand, rolling through Savannah's streets, listening to stories about eerie hauntings. Most of these embellished tales had a tiny speck of truth to them. Savannah's colorful past had resulted in several mysterious disappearances, and the ghosts of both pirates and socialites kept some of the locals unnerved for years.

Settling back at her desk, she checked to see if she had a message from Jack. He was in London at the International Bar Association Conference, and their time differences had been affecting their chats. Her eyes focused on a new message, but once she read the words McMillon Farms, everything began to spin. She held on to the desk tightly until the feeling passed. Twenty-eight years should have been plenty of time to brace herself for that moment, but she was still unprepared. Her hands shook as she slowly opened the message and pictured, for a brief second, the man who had written it. "WE MUST TALK. Quinn"

# THE SECRET EXPOSED

KNOCK, COUNTY MAYO, IRELAND

Quinn sat on the back patio, gazing over the fields, knowing that his life had instantly changed forever. He watched the barley sway in the April breezes as if God's hand was running softly across the stalks. The sight usually calmed him, but Sundays were always emotional for him. Oh, how he wished Maura was there. More than a year had passed since her death. Yet, when he closed his eyes, he could feel her presence. In those moments, the brain and heart forget time.

His Sunday had started just like every other Sunday: 11 o'clock Mass at Our Lady of Knock followed by the trip back to the farm to await the dinner bell. Each Sunday, the girls did their best to continue their late mother's ritual, and even though their meals weren't quite as tasty, the company was always comforting. When the McMillon family were all together, love and happiness prevailed.

His daughter, Colleen, had dropped by before Mass and put a large pot of Irish Stew in the oven. The savory onion and beef aroma began to fill the air making Quinn's stomach growl. Like her mother, Colleen didn't allow grazing, so Quinn knew better than to sneak a sample before the meal was entirely cooked and served.

Reflecting on the homily from the morning Mass, Quinn remembered that Father had spoken of choices. Simple choices can be chocolate or vanilla, or more difficult choices could be deciding on a career or choosing a spouse. Each choice, no matter how simple or complex, affects the future. Something about that one sentence made Quinn think of Kathleen. Quinn's mind drifted to that morning 30 years ago when she left to go back to the states. His stomach tightened with guilt, but he reasoned with himself, *We were so young and from different worlds. It never would have worked out.* He gazed out on the fields again and opened his laptop. *I wonder how she is? Is she happy?*

A few years back, Maura thought Facebook would be an excellent way to keep up with family, so they had joined under the name McMillon Farms. He put in a search for the name "Kathleen Kenny," and in an instant, the computer screen flooded with faces of Kathleens from all over the world, but none looked remotely familiar. Quinn was putting away the laptop when thoughts from the morning homily made him continue. Laughing at himself, he made a choice. *What the heck, one more try.* So he was more specific and typed in "Kathleen Kenny, Savannah, Georgia." A single face appeared with a different last name. Kathleen Kenny Murray. Although she was an older version of the Kathleen he knew, she looked the same and still had that twinkle in her eye. "Still up to mischief, I bet," he mumbled out loud. "That was a lifetime ago when things were different."

He started looking at her Facebook info. His children called that "stalking," but he figured it was getting reacquainted. *I wonder if she married that American bloke and how she's keeping these days?* His eyes focused on one particular family picture. He tried to move, to breathe, or to talk but was utterly stunned. Finally, he gasped, "THIS CAN'T BE!" as Colleen stepped onto the patio.

"Da! What's wrong?" she asked and ran to his side.

Quinn sat frozen, still staring at the computer screen. "What have you done?" he mumbled in confusion, and then reality hit. "Kathleen, what have you done?"

Colleen dropped her glass of wine on the patio; it shattered to pieces. The sound stunned Quinn, and he noticed her standing there for the first time. Looking over his shoulder, Colleen narrowed her gaze at the screen, "Da, how can this be?"

# FINDING STRENGTH

Kathleen sat on the stone bench in the garden, staring aimlessly into the fountain, deep in thought. She had sent word to Jack and tried to mentally prepare a conversation that she had hoped to suspend indefinitely. The garden always gave her security. She believed in decorating with well-loved things. Through the years, she and Jack had combined the three things they loved the most: their trips to Italy, their Catholic faith, and their love of old Savannah. They added something special from each of these and put them all together in their garden.

People must have liked the wacky combination because "peekers" always looked through the iron gates trying to catch a glimpse of the garden. In other cities, that might be odd, but that was part of the charm and beauty of their fair city. People walked the brick sidewalks, day and night, gazing into the gardens of downtown homes. Each person found their favorite gardens to walk by and peek into, and surprisingly enough, at each passing, their eyes found something new – like magic. Now that her boys were older, she was able to enjoy the "peekers" without fear that they might see more than they bargained for with her rambunctious band of heathens. Her son Philip was famous on Jones Street for his natural watering of her azaleas; the boy had no shame.

She gazed up to the statue of Saint Michael the Archangel in the center of their fountain. On their last trip to Rome, their family had stayed in a townhome across the Tiber River from Castel Sant' Angelo. A statue of the Archangel Michael stood at the top of the castle, protecting all of Rome. It was said that Saint Michael appeared during the time of the plague, sheathing his bloody sword from the battle, as the plague disappeared in fear. Pope St. Gregory the Great created a statue to remember Saint Michael. Their children knew the Saint Michael prayer well because they recited it daily in Catholic grade school. Every time a member of their family passed the garden fountain, there was a whisper of, "Saint Michael the Archangel, defend us in battle, be our protection against the wickedness and snares of the devil. May God rebuke him…" The fountain faced their home and watched over all who dwelt inside.

She would need that protection in her battle ahead.

Her ringing phone stirred her back to reality, and she quickly felt the warmth of Jack's voice. After telling him about her message from Quinn, he was direct with his request. "I'll be home in five days. Just sit tight until then. Don't even answer his message until we talk face to face. Promise me?" Jack asked.

"I promise!" she answered.

"Not even to the tribe," he said. "You know it's going to be hard at lunch tomorrow since you tell them everything, but please respect this and keep it to yourself."

"I promise," she repeated.

The tribe met for lunch every Wednesday at 11:30, each of the six taking a turn to select the spot, which had to be within the Savannah city limits. This week it was Maggie's pick. She was going through a martini phase, so she had chosen The Shrimp Factory on River Street because it had both a bar and excellent shrimp and grits.

Through the years, they remained each other's lifeline. They had been in each other's weddings – some more than once – at baptisms, birthday parties, hospital stays, and graduations. They laughed together and cried together. People say that each person in the world needs a tribe of friends to help them succeed, and they were each other's tribe. Their group texts constantly rang from sunup to sundown and sometimes in between.

Over time, they had come up with many unwritten by-laws. They agreed to always be truthful with one another, even when it was difficult. They also vowed not to gossip about one another to other group members. They tried not to talk about people outside the group too, but when the six women got together with drinks in hand, they frequently forgot that rule. Their latest by-law was that they couldn't do anything that could land them in jail. This was added after they took a late-night sprint running from the cops after putting sugar in the gas tank of a cheating boyfriend. No good could come from all of them being sent up the river.

Kathleen knew that she had not been truthful, and to top it off, she was the world's worst liar. She'd only lied to them one other time: the week after Thomas' appendectomy. Everyone had assumed she was out of sorts because of the surgery, so no one caught her in the lie. She prayed that this week would be as easy.

Her afternoon dragged by as she repeatedly played out every scenario on how things would end. All of her worries melted into a long night of distress. She had finally fallen to sleep in her favorite chair in the living room just as the traces of morning light began to show through the blinds. The booming sound of her hardback book hitting her hardwood floors startled her awake at 10 o'clock. She shot up. Trying to take a deep breath, she placed her fingers on the artery under her jaw, thankful when the beats went back to normal. *This is how my day is going to be,* she thought and shook her head in disbelief. Being so far off of her usual morning schedule, she barely made it out of the door in time for her lunch date with the tribe.

As she balanced on the cobblestones walking to River Street, she stumbled along the ballast that had been deposited onto the wharf long ago from seafaring ships. *If only these stones could talk. They probably have just as many secrets as me,* she said to herself. She tripped a second time and wondered why she was having such a tough time walking on the uneven rocks. She was completely preoccupied but made herself focus on The Shrimp Factory's red and white striped awning.

Upon entering the restaurant, she was taken in by the nautical atmosphere. The hardwood floors and combination of exposed brick and shiplap walls gave the restaurant a cozy vibe. Instantly she heard her friends' distinct loud voices coming from the front room, which overlooked the Savannah River. She followed the noise until they came into view. Each one of them was wearing a birthday hat as they excitedly talked over the other. She mentally began going over everyone's birthday, wondering whose special day she had missed. Maggie walked towards her yelling, "Happy

Anniversary!" and presented her with a cup of potent Chatham Artillery Punch, a Savannah cocktail made with several jiggers of liquor. She started to put a hat on Kathleen's head but stopped in midair, looked her over, then tentatively continued to place the hat onto Kathleen's unruly hair. Maggie looked worriedly at Stephanie, Agnes, and Jan, who were already seated at the table, and nodded towards Kathleen as she helped her to the table. Latrice was the last to arrive. She surveyed the group, and her eyes honed in on Kathleen. "What in the hell happened to you?"

"What do you mean?" Kathleen asked.

"You look like you were just hit by a bus. When's the last time you brushed your hair? Do you realize you have on two different shoes? And, what in the world are you wearing?"

Kathleen looked down at herself and was mortified. "I'm just having a bad day – well, in all honesty – a bad couple of days."

"You don't have "bad days." Are Jack and the kids okay?"

"Yes, yes. Everyone is fine." Kathleen quickly ran her fingers through her hair and changed the discussion. "So Maggie, what are we celebrating?"

Maggie tentatively started the conversation, still worrying about Kathleen. But, as usual, her enthusiasm soon kicked in. "Judging from the looks on your faces, you probably don't remember, but today marks the 28th anniversary of our first tribe lunch."

"Are we really that old? I still think of myself as being in my thirties," Stephanie spit out immediately. "When I think of our initial tribe lunch, I picture us being kids, but we were adults already making decisions about our futures."

"But some of us didn't anticipate the consequences of those decisions," Kathleen groaned, staring down into her drink. Everyone looked questioningly to one another, each wondering if she was referring to them.

Maggie kept the conversation going, "Hush now and listen. I figured this out last night. We started meeting the year we all came back to town from college while planning Kathleen's wedding. It's been 28 years of us meeting once a week. That's 1,456 meals together."

"Whoa! That would explain all of those extra pounds on my derriere," Agnes said.

"Ladies," Maggie continued, "Not many people can say they've had that many meals with five of their best friends and closest confidants. We are so very blessed, so I thought we should celebrate."

Jan jumped in saying, "Well, you must really want to celebrate if you ordered us all Chatham Artillery Punch. We all know they call it 'punch' for a reason. Need I remind y'all of drinking punch at the July 4th party?" Everyone groaned.

"Only one for me," said Latrice. "And you better still carry around those potent little breath mints that cover the smell. They are expecting me back at work."

"Latrice gets a pass...this time, but the rest of you have no excuse. Now raise your glasses. This toast is to our tribe," and Maggie finished off drink number one.

"To the tribe!" they all said in unison.

Thankfully, their orders came out quickly before drink number two was placed in front of each of them, without being asked. Lunch had been prepared from fresh local seafood, right out of the Atlantic Ocean. As Maggie's dad, the shrimper, said, "You know it's fresh when it's swimming one day, and you're eating it the next." Fried shrimp, red snapper tacos, shrimp and grits, seafood gumbo, and crab cake sandwiches filled the table. They enjoyed their meal in the comfort of friends who knew everything about one another. Well, almost everything.

They ended their lunch the same way they did every week. The Mistress of Ceremonies, whom they called the "MC," was the person who had selected the restaurant and covered the bill. After it was paid, the tribe gave the "MC" a score based on three categories: meal, service, and the Grand Slam. The last category was reserved for something extraordinary. The maximum score was five, but those were seldom given. The "MC" with the most points at the end of the year was awarded a time-honored trophy and a small shopping spree on Broughton Street, courtesy of the other five.

Although Ted, the waiter, had been super nice, he lost his patience with the group before their meals had been served. The food was magnificent, which made up for Ted's sour disposition, but the Grand Slam was not even considered. At the end of lunch, and after three attempts to get them to leave, Ted hit the breaking point, addressing Maggie. "Ma'am. Excuse me, Ma'am? I believe you're ignoring me on purpose, and we need to give our staff time between shifts to regroup for dinner. Can you and your party please make your way towards the door? God bless your husband." Maggie seemed upset, suddenly noticing that they were the only patrons left in the restaurant. She hurriedly gathered her things and shooed everyone to the door. As they stepped into the blinding sun, reflected upon the bright white oyster shells of the tabby sidewalk, Maggie exclaimed, "Well, shit fire!"

"What in the world is wrong?" Stephanie asked, thinking that Ted's husband jab must have hurt her feelings.

"I'll never win that trophy!" She shouted, and they all

burst out laughing. Maggie was the only one in the group who had never won the trophy. Everyone knew that she was a waiter's worst nightmare, but she always got an A for effort.

Kathleen felt the weight of Latrice's stare, and tried not to make eye contact. Latrice quickly called her out, "We didn't forget about you, and you're not off the hook yet. We all know something is wrong and are here for you if you need us. All you gotta do is ask." Kathleen smiled slightly and nodded because she knew just how special her friends were and was relieved that they weren't going to pry any further.

They said their goodbyes on the sidewalk and went in separate directions. Kathleen huffed and puffed up the steep incline of the cobblestone ramp. When she finally made it to the top, she decided to walk along Bay Street and found herself sitting on a bench in Emmet Park, staring at the Celtic Cross. Her Irish roots ran deep, and her heart held many connections to Ireland. Her mind took her back to the day that she wandered around Kylemore Abbey in County Galway and the several Celtic Crosses that dotted the property. She had been all alone that day, too, but she had felt such peace. Oh, how she wished she could find that peace again. She looked back up at the stone cross in front of her and closed her eyes, laboring to draw upon those feelings. She thought about the year she had gone to Ireland. That was the same year she had married Jack, and the year she was pregnant with Thomas.

# CHASING THE WIND

30 Years Before

Kathleen knew from an early age that she was different than everyone else. When she read fairy tales, she could feel the cold from the castle stones and could picture looking out over the vast English countryside through the eyes of the princess. As she grew older, she realized that her thoughts held the reality of distant places she had never been.

In her desire to be an average teenager, she hid her abilities and quickly learned how to conceal them. But more so than that, she knew how to control her feelings. It was easy during the day but what she couldn't control was her sleep, and that had become the avenue her mind used. Her dreams had power over her will, and they used that advantage to take her to that one place – to Ireland – the land of her ancestors.

Kathleen's parents were born to Irish immigrants. Her great-grandfather, Harry Kenny, once lived in Knock,

Ireland, where Our Lady appeared on August 21, 1879. On the anniversary of that date, her grandfather would come to their house for dinner every year. He would begin the evening by reading mysteriously from an old tattered journal that had belonged to his father. Like most Irish storytellers, he made the worn-out journal come alive. He left his audience, made up of his wee little Irish grandkids, wanting more.

This tradition continued after his passing. Her dad now read to them from the same tattered journal. They would pray a family rosary and enjoy a delicious dinner of corned beef and cabbage, with a side of Irish Soda Bread.

Her father would end the evening explaining, "In the 1800s, Savannah's Old Fort neighborhood was filled with working-class Irish families. They named their nearby park "Irish Green," in remembrance of their homeland. That park has since been renamed Emmet Park. There's a Celtic Cross in its center honoring Americans of Irish descent. Don't ever forget where you came from," he stressed while wagging his finger at the group. Then, just like a pirate whispering where he buried his treasure, he would mutter, "Let's go see it." And they would pile in the car and ride down to Bay Street.

Although Kathleen's dreams weren't about apparitions or rosaries, they were about Ireland…that of which she was sure. The dream was always the same…she was walking past a long stone wall, between fields and a small stream. She could feel a breeze on her face and smell the rich soil in the air. She was searching for something but not knowing what. *Where is it?* She would think to herself. *Where?* She looked everywhere but was nervous about what she might find. She would wake up, the same as always, with a strange prickle down the back of her neck and lingering confusion, like her brain was still in the place she had visited.

This particular day was no exception. She sat up in bed and glanced at the clock that read 6:30 a.m. *What was I searching for?* She asked herself, still in a foggy haze. Her family was vacationing on nearby Tybee Island. She knew that she was up for the day and needed to clear her mind before driving the two-lane Tybee road back to town. She took a brisk walk down to the beach as the sun slowly crept its way into the sky. The growing light of day chased off all of the darkness from the previous night, giving her the clarity she needed.

After her walk, Kathleen tiptoed back into their rented summer house. She quietly stepped over her siblings, who had fallen asleep the night before in front of the television while watching "Shark Week." Smiling to herself, she pictured them spending the day at the beach in fear, trying to swim in ankle-deep water.

Tybee is an island with lovely salt-water creeks and marshlands, but its pride and joy is the mile-and-a-half long beach. During the summer, people flock to the sandy shores to sunbathe and play in the surf. Nineteen numbered streets lead right into the sand, but there was only one street for high school and college students, and that was 10th Street. From 11 a.m. until way after 11 p.m., 10th Street was the place to be. It was where everyone gathered with friends to enjoy time off from school. It was also where everyone caught up on gossip that was missed during the summer. Hot topics were always who's dating who, who's not dating anymore, and who wished they could find a date. Birdwell's and bikinis were a must!!!

Kathleen's parents were strong advocates of their teenage

children having the responsibility of jobs. But as she grew older, she realized that raising a large family was expensive, so she was always happy to work. Her siblings found part-time positions on Tybee, but she continued her year-round job at Leopold's Ice Cream Parlor in downtown Savannah.

She was sad leaving Tybee that morning, but her spirits soon lifted as her car approached the Lazaretto Creek Bridge. She loved the drive from Tybee into town, and it was just what she needed to pull her away from last night's dream. As she drove, she turned up the radio, rolled down her windows, and chased the wind with her hand. Her world was soon transformed. The smell of asphalt was chased away by the muddy scent of salt-water marsh. Some days, if she were lucky, she might spot a dolphin swimming along the bank as it pushed shrimp up into the mud. This particular day, it was already hotter than Hades, but she just couldn't force herself to roll up the windows. How could she miss out on the breeze and smells of her favorite stretch of road in the whole world: Tybee to Savannah . . . her heaven!

Kathleen attended Armstrong State College in Savannah and had just completed her junior year. When she wasn't scooping up delicious ice cream that had a four-minute life-span in the Georgia heat, she hung out with friends who were home for the summer. She loved her friends and enjoyed hearing of their many adventures off at school, but sometimes she couldn't help but wonder when she would have some adventure of her own.

Then it happened. Kathleen was enjoying a shrimp salad sandwich while sunbathing in Johnson Square during her lunch break. She noticed Jack circling the square looking to park his Ford pickup. Everyone who had attended Benedictine or St. Vincent's (Savannah's Catholic high schools) knew

Jack. He was a big-shot football player who helped take the BC Cadets to the state championship three years in a row. After high school, he planned to attend the University of Georgia. Everyone knew he would be playing ball for the Georgia Bulldogs and was shocked when he decided to concentrate on his academics and end his football career. Obviously, it was a good choice because he had just graduated from UGA's School of Law and landed a job working for a prominent law firm downtown.

She watched Jack cursing and yanking on the steering wheel as he tried to parallel park his clunky Ford truck. She tried not to stare and return to peaceful sunbathing in the square, but the line of cars and horn honking disturbed her relaxation hour. On Jack's third attempt, she walked up and banged on the hood of his truck, just as he was unsuccessfully inching his way in reverse. When he rolled down the window she said, "I'll bet you $10.00 I can park this truck my first try."

He laughed and said, "No way," and motioned his hand as if to shoo her away.

"Suit yourself, but take a look behind you." A line of cars was waiting, with drivers growing angrier by the second. He rolled his eyes and slid over to the passenger seat. Two parking spots were available on the square, and Jack struggled to maneuver the truck into the larger spot. Kathleen pulled out, moved towards the smaller spot, passed it three-quarters of the way, threw the truck in reverse, turned the wheel just right, and gunned it into the smaller spot. He rolled his eyes a second time and pulled out his wallet saying, "St. Vincent's girl, right?"

The young ladies who attended St. Vincent's Academy were known for many things, some good and some not so good. But the one skill they all mastered was parallel parking. St. Vincent's was the only high school in the downtown area where parking places were scarce. Parallel parking skills were essential when finding one of those coveted spots on a school morning. Many drivers would wait, hoping the driver couldn't accomplish the task, so they could try.

As the line of angry drivers was finally able to pass, waving their fists at Jack, Kathleen turned to him with a smirk and claimed her $10 reward.

"I don't like to lose," he said.

"Too bad," she said as she stepped out of the truck, leaned in the open window and added, "You just did!"

Jack grinned and watched her walk across the park, saying under his breath, "Please look back, please look back, if she's interested, she'll look back." When she did, their eyes locked, and a huge smile spread across his face.

That afternoon, she was at work making a milkshake for an older downtown resident when Jack walked into Leopold's. He stood there grinning, like the cat who had swallowed the canary, and she knew she was done for. He was so handsome, but he didn't seem to realize it and instead focused all of his attention on other people. Today that focus was on her. He waited patiently in line while she served customers, but she could feel his eyes burning on her. When he finally got his turn, she tried to be very calm, "May I help you, sir?"

"Kathleen? Rumor has it that you are whipping up the best milkshakes this side of Bay Street."

"Well, if I'm serving them, you know they're the best." She wondered how he knew her name but then remembered the name tag she was wearing. "What flavor can I get you?"

"Chocolate, of course. What time do you get off?" he

asked. A group of girls standing behind him in line all began to giggle. He looked back in surprise and suddenly seemed embarrassed. He blushed at the scrutiny of the teenage girls, and it made her smile.

"I hope you don't rattle that easily in a courtroom," she laughed. "I get off in 10 minutes."

"Can I buy you dinner tonight? I think that I owe you since you helped me out of my parking disaster. We can go anywhere you'd like."

Her stomach fluttered with thoughts of sitting with Jack at dinner. Suddenly, she felt self-conscious and blushed. "I'd like that. Elizabeth's on 37th Street. Pick me up at 7 o'clock. Better make a reservation; your luck isn't very good."

"See you tonight," Jack said as he walked toward the door yelling back over his shoulder, "My luck's about to change."

## BEST FRIENDS

Kathleen told the tribe about her date with Jack the following night when they met at Stephanie's house on the Wilmington River. From the second they laid eyes on her, they knew she had a secret and continued to pry until she came clean. Kathleen appeared to be telling a fairy tale when they all plopped down in the chairs and gave her their full attention. They laughed that Kathleen parallel parked Jack's truck and were intrigued that he searched her out at the ice cream shop to ask her for a date. Everyone was in love with Jack by the time he had kissed Kathleen goodnight after a romantic dinner. "I have never, ever felt such a connection to anyone," she admitted, "but y'all know my plans. After graduation, I'm taking off. I've been stuck in Savannah for far too long. I've been looking at Price Waterhouse in Atlanta and other big accounting firms in Jacksonville. I'm not ready to be tied down. Not yet." She instantly felt relief from putting her fears into words and the love and familiarity of being with close friends.

It always had been just the six of them. At times, other people floated in and out, but the six remained constant. They were from all parts of Savannah and from all walks of life, and yet they had one thing in common that bonded them on that last day in August when freshman year of high school began: FEAR. The school's mascot was a Saint, but most of the upperclassmen were anything but saintly. That morning, each had been pushed around while looking for classrooms and lockers, then shoved to the back of the lunch line while every senior took a "senior cut" to the front. By the time they all picked up their food, they sat at the only empty spot left in the gym: the table at the end. It was the six of them sitting together that day, and every school day after, until graduation.

Back at Stephanie's house, all six of them quietly thought about Kathleen's fear of falling in love. Maggie was the first to speak, "We ARE talking Jack Murray, right? THE Jack Murray? The Jack Murray that we all were gaga about in high school?"

Stephanie interrupted, "Looks aren't everything, Maggie. But he seems to be much more than a hunk. He's nice, and he's a lawyer…just saying."

Latrice piped in, "Jack isn't asking you to marry him. So, at this point, you should just enjoy yourself and see where it goes. Did he ask you for another date?"

Kathleen timidly answered, "Yes, for tonight, but I told him that I had plans with y'all." They all burst out laughing, telling her she was crazy to miss a date with Jack. She instantly felt better in the company of her friends. They talked and laughed until after midnight, then they all ran down to the dock and jumped into the river. Climbing out, each found a spot on the side of the dock to dangle their feet in the water. Thankful for the full moon, Kathleen noticed the moonlight flickering on the blue gems of their Saint Vincent's Academy rings. She then looked at her tribe, one by one.

Agnes was on a basketball scholarship at Notre Dame and would graduate in the spring with a business degree. Her eyes drifted over to Latrice. She was a brilliant, die-hard bookworm and was preparing to graduate from an international college in London.

Maggie interrupted Kathleen's thoughts by splashing saltwater in her face. "Why so serious? Let's have fun!" Maggie was a cheerleader at Georgia Southern College and was both perky and energetic. She could lift anyone out of a bad mood. Maggie's Dad was a shrimper, and she grew up on the many waterways in Savannah. She swam like a fish, so Kathleen wasn't surprised when Maggie climbed up on the dock rail and performed a perfect backflip. She continued to float on her back and began spitting saltwater up onto Jan's hanging legs.

Jan laughed, saying, "Six girls were just swimming in that murky water. I'm sure that one or more of us might have peed a little; hope you enjoy that in your mouth." They all yelled "GROSS!" except Maggie, who shrugged and dove under the water. Jan was the artist in the group and was funky and totally out there. She usually saw things much different from the other five, which always gave a new perspective. Her art hung in galleries and restaurants throughout Savannah.

Kathleen looked past Jan to Stephanie. As always, she was busy fixing something, and tonight it was one of the dock cleats. Next spring, she would be graduating from Georgia

Tech and had a job lined up with the Corp of Engineers in downtown Savannah.

When they realized Maggie had been underwater for a long time, they all started to sit up a little more and look for bubbles in the brown-gray water. As usual, all eyes turned to Kathleen to see if they should be alarmed when suddenly Maggie grabbed Stephanie's ankles and pulled her in. Everyone stood up and jumped in, too. Kathleen had been the one they had nicknamed "Mom." Being the oldest of six children, three of them boys, Kathleen had seen it all. She also was a good listener, so everyone came to her with their problems.

They sat on the dock and talked until early morning. Although they each had such love for one another, Kathleen felt left out of many of their conversations, complaining about bad roommates, traveling around the world, and being homesick. She looked forward to her time after graduation when she could experience some of those same things. Then she thought about something her Dad had told her years ago. "Savannah is like a magnet, you can leave, but it always pulls you back. Just like the river ebbs and flows, true Savannahians always come home." She had prayed that it was true and that her friends would return to Savannah after graduation, but she also wondered if she would be there when they did.

# HOITY TOITY

After Kathleen and Jack's first date, they spent every free minute together. He drove down to Tybee every night after work, asking if he could eat with her family. Kathleen watched his face light up when he was in the middle of her family chaos. He teased her younger siblings just like they were his own, and he always helped her Mom put the food on the table. Whenever her dad was grilling, Jack was at his side drinking a beer, and they would talk to one another like old friends.

Kathleen had dated several guys, but none of them actually had wanted to be with her family. She immediately let her guard down with Jack. He was asked to family dinners and was included at the July 4th party. Her dad even turned his head when he caught them necking on the front porch.

Many nights after dinner, they would go alone to swim in the surf on the numbered streets, float in the Back River, take long walks on the beach after dark, and make out in the sand dunes. She was amazed how being near him could excite her and longed for his touch when they were apart.

One night, as they swung in the hammock on the porch of the beach house, he asked her to come to his house to have dinner with his parents. "I'd like you to meet my Mom and dad. I can leave work a little early on Friday and come down to pick you up," he said.

She nodded, "Sure, I'd like that." As they continued to sway, she thought how wonderful it would be to meet his parents. Jack was the kindest and happiest person she had ever met, so his parents must be exceptional people. She could hardly wait until Friday.

Jack picked Kathleen up after work. He was still in his business suit, but she wore a sleeveless shirt, shorts, and sandals. She had spent the day on the beach with the tribe, and the sting of the sun was glowing on her face. He smiled when she opened the door and pulled her in close. "You look like summer in a package." Then he nuzzled his nose into her neck, "You even smell like coconuts." His work-day stubble tickled, and she was giggling so loud that they didn't hear her dad walk up behind her. "Keep it PG, you two, little eyes are everywhere," he said with ease as Jack backed away. The two men shook hands and regarded each other with mutual affection.

As they drove off of Tybee and into town, she suddenly realized that she didn't know where he lived. She had never even asked. He had always been on her turf, so she selfishly figured it wasn't important. The longer they were in the car, the more her curiosity had peaked, until it was more than she could withstand. Finally, she broke down and asked, "So, where do you live, Jack?"

"The Landings," he answered.

Kathleen had always thought of The Landings as being hoity-toity. It was a large gated community on Skidaway

Island with several golf courses and country clubs and a big mean guard who wouldn't let anyone in who didn't belong. She knew this because she and the tribe had tried to go to The Landings for a party last year. The guard wouldn't raise that damn entry gate, and they were stuck with cars behind them and no way to proceed. The guard sat there, with his arms crossed and a smirk on his face, as they shamefully asked the cars behind them to back up so they could make their getaway. She had grown up with a family that believed that you build bridges, not walls and that everyone was equal. The thought of a gate to keep the unwanted out was both unnecessary and offensive. However, the older she became, she realized that it was only offensive to the people on the outside of the gate.

As they approached his ritzy subdivision, lo and behold, the same guard from last year was on duty. This time he didn't wear a smirk. "Hello, Mr. Murray," he said. "I hope that you had a nice day." Then he leaned over to nod at her.

She looked him in the eye, smiled real big, and gave him the finger. She wasn't sure if it was recognition or disdain that flashed across his face, but the guard drew back as if someone had slapped him. Automatically Jack looked to her to see why, but she had pasted on a sweet smile and was giving her best Southern girl wave by the time he turned. She rubbed Jack's arm as they entered the development's lovely grounds, knowing she would be the first person in the confessional on Saturday.

Kathleen felt her stomach tighten and said a little prayer to calm her nerves. They drove along the winding roads, passing people on golf carts, kids riding bikes, and dozens of workers maintaining the grounds. Finally, Jack pulled into a driveway of what she had thought was one of the clubs, but actually was his house. WHOA! How did she not know Jack came from money? He never acted like someone with money. She knew wealthy people and usually could spot them from a mile away, judging by how they carried themselves. Jack wasn't like that at all. To put it frankly, she was shocked.

As Jack casually opened the massive front doors, like he had done his whole life, she realized that she was entering into a world very different from her own. A maid greeted them and asked them to go into the bar for a drink with his parents. What? They had their own bar. And more importantly, a maid? *Toto, we're not in Kansas anymore,* she thought.

The knot in her stomach tightened as they walked through the house, and when they turned the corner into the bar, she realized why. His parents were sitting on a settee, having a drink of what they called a mint julep. Jack introduced her, and she instantly felt his mother's eyes giving her a good once over. His father was a big man with a huge presence and was very nice. He walked right up to her and gave her a hug. She liked him immediately, but she wasn't sure about his Mom. She was standoffish and appeared to be deep in thought. She was wearing a sundress, pearls, and pumps. The best word to describe her was "classy."

"Are y'all going out after dinner?" Kathleen asked. "You look lovely."

His Mom seemed confused, looking down at herself and back to Kathleen. "No dear, like most families in Savannah, we dress for dinner."

Bam, there it was. Insult number one. Kathleen nervously nodded her head up and down but realized she had continued nodding and made herself stop. She knew that she must look like the village idiot, but she had absolutely nothing to say to Jack's parents.

Without being asked, she was served a mint julep, which tasted like toothpaste. Kathleen's stomach growled out loud when the maid walked in with a silver platter piled high with little hors d'oeuvres. Mr. Murray laughed with a genuine happy laugh, but Mrs. Murray simply said, "Hmmmm."

They were summoned to dinner by the ring of a tiny bell. It was almost laughable compared to her family's style. Her Mom would yell, "Dinner time," and they would run to the table. She suddenly wished her Mom were there. She drew upon the strength from that thought and reminded herself that these were Jack's parents and that he was amazing. They were just people, and she would start talking to them like she would her parents.

They walked into a sizable cranberry-colored room furnished with an antique cherry table set with Spode Delamere Cranberry fine china and crystal stemware. His dad sat at the head, with his Mom and Kathleen on each side and Jack to her right. Suddenly three people began serving dinner and bringing out dishes. She looked at each of Jack's parents waiting for the blessing, but instead, they picked up the correct fork and started eating. She and Jack had shared many meals together and attended 5:30 Mass on Tybee, so she knew he was Catholic, but now she began questioning his upbringing. She bowed her head and closed her eyes, made the sign of the cross, and silently said the blessing. As she finished with the sign of the cross again, she looked up, and both Mr. and Mrs. Murray's forks were frozen in midair. Jack, however, had a huge smile on his face and gave a booming, "Amen!"

Mr. Murray began talking business with Jack about

things she had no idea about and honestly didn't even care to learn. That gave his Mom an open playing field to interrogate Kathleen, "So Kathleen, what is it that you do?"

"I'm in business school at Armstrong studying to be an accountant."

"I've never heard of a female accountant before," Mrs. Murray said condescendingly. "Do you intend to work in an office with all males for the rest of your life?"

Kathleen looked at her with complete confusion at the stupidity of that question, smiled, then answered, "I'm really good with numbers and am tutoring half of the boys in my classes. I'm not intending to work side by side with an office full of males for the rest of my life. I'm planning to be their boss."

Mrs. Murray smirked and began to talk about all the prominent accountant's wives that she knew. She droned on and on about their children and their many accolades. Kathleen was nervous, and her mouth became parched. She was struggling to swallow a piece of chicken and suddenly realized that she couldn't breathe. She was choking. Before she understood what was happening, Jack had grabbed her from behind and was doing the Heimlich Maneuver. His dad screamed for someone to call 911, the staff was hysterical, but his mother sat motionless at the table. The only thing that Kathleen remembered was the look on his Mom's face when the chicken flew into the air and landed right into her soup bowl.

On the drive back to Tybee, Kathleen was uncharacteristically quiet. When Jack reached over to hold her hand, she burst out in tears. "Oh My Gosh! A piece of chicken flew from my mouth and into your mother's soup bowl. How did that happen? She has to hate me."

"Are you kidding me? You almost died tonight, and you are worried about my Mom? I was terrified when you were choking. What if I couldn't have saved you?" Then he glanced over at Kathleen. She looked so frail and disheartened, so he talked softly. "My Mom doesn't hate you. It's no big deal."

"She didn't seem too pleased with me from the minute we got to your house; the chunk of chicken in her soup bowl just sealed the deal."

"It's not that she doesn't like you; she just wasn't expecting you. She has been trying to set me up with different Savannah debutantes, from the Junior League, for as long as I can remember. You are a breath of fresh air."

She nodded slowly. "Jack, you come from a different world than I do. You come from maids and clubs, and I come from kids doing chores and digging holes in the yard."

"Didn't you know that I came from a wealthy family?" he asked.

"No, I had no idea."

"And that's why we work. Everyone else I have dated knew my family had lots of money long before we went out. You just assumed I didn't and were good with that. You like me for me, and I definitely like you, and I love how you live out your faith. You inspire me to become stronger in mine. Don't worry, Kate, my Mom will loosen up, you'll see."

Kathleen was surprised when Jack called her Kate. It warmed her heart at how intimate it felt, but more importantly, it seemed to make all of her worries disappear.

# THE SOCIALITE

Teresa Murray shut the door behind Jack as he and Kathleen walked to their car. She gently laid her head against the door and closed her eyes. This night had not been what she had expected. When Jack graduated from law school, she knew it was time to start pulling her strings to find the right wife for her son. However, he was less than enthused with her choices and changed the subject every time she brought up his future.

During the summer, Jack began putting in more and more hours at his job and coming home every night extremely late. One morning, when he was walking out the door, he asked if he could bring someone home for dinner. He had never done that before, and she was on cloud nine. Obviously, one of her matches took because he had been working far too many hours to find somebody new. She was thrilled and hummed all day as she prepared for the evening.

The Murrays employed a staff of three, all of whom had been the outcome of sad legal cases that Roger had worked on. Each had begged for a job so they could take care of their families. They had become like family and helped her maintain the overly large house that the Murrays were expected to own. They all adored Jack and wanted the night to be perfect for him.

Then Kathleen entered Teresa's life. She was pretty, but more than that, she was smart. If Jack were an ordinary man, Kathleen would have been her first pick. But he was following in his Dad's footsteps and most certainly was not ordinary. She battled with her feelings all night, and now that they were alone, she finally discussed them with Roger.

"I like her," Roger said the second the door shut behind them. His voice startled her, and she slowly lifted her eyes off the door and turned to look at him.

"I do, too, but . . ."

"You do not. You might as well have been sucking lemons all night."

"I do. I just...Roger, she puked on the dining room table. I know she was choking, but I just don't know . . I guess I just wanted more for Jack."

"More what?"

"I don't know. Just more. I've mapped out Jack's life for him in my head, and she doesn't fit into my plan." She rubbed her temples and shook her head, "I can honestly say, I've never seen Jack look like he did tonight. He loves her, Roger. Couldn't take his eyes off of her and hung on her every word." Teresa had to keep moving to clear her mind. She had felt the cry in her throat and didn't want to give into it, so she started cleaning up from dinner. After everything was put away, she slipped into bed and snuggled next to Roger, who was reading.

He rubbed her head and said, "Kathleen is good for Jack. Know what? She reminds me of someone." He hesitated for a moment, then proceeded slowly. "She's bright and strong-willed." He stopped talking, and Teresa turned her face up towards his. Roger kissed the end of her nose. "Do you remember the first time we met?" She nodded, but he stayed focused as if he were reliving a memory that had to be re-told. "You were sitting on a bench in Johnson Square at lunch, reading a book. You were always reading your books. I was cutting through the park and had stopped to tie my shoe beside your bench. You looked up from your book, and when our eyes met, I became nervous and blurted out, "I just came from the courthouse. I have a big case. Do you remember what you said?"

She was embarrassed but answered, "I said, Men who carry a big briefcase are compensating. Big briefcase…little brain."

He belly laughed, and she started to laugh, too. "I remember thinking that you were both pretty and smart, and that was a dangerous combination. Then I explained how I had a big COURT case, not a big BRIEF case."

"And I was shocked because so many men didn't understand my sense of humor. You had a twinkle in your eye that made it look like you were amused at something. You still have it, you know?" She smiled and cuddled in closer. "We were married less than a year later."

"It's no wonder Jack is in love. She's got spunk, like you, and she wasn't trying to impress either of us. She will hold up just fine with the Savannah elite. And if she doesn't, she will be just fine without them."

She laid her head in the crook of his shoulder until his breathing slowed to just shy of a snore. Processing what he said, she knew that it would never be that easy because she had lived through Savannah's snobbery firsthand. During all of the miscarriages, Roger had been right at her side. He had cried through each one with her, year after year. But he had to keep working, socializing, and putting on a happy face. She quickly realized that not one of those people she was associating with ever came to check on her. All of those times she had hosted them for luncheons and showers were because they were getting something out of it. That's when the bitterness started to set in.

Teresa slowly turned out of Roger's arm and onto her left side and sighed quietly. They had crushed her so much that she had to pull away from everyone before she was destroyed. But as Jack became older, she made herself re-enter those dreaded social circles so that Jack would have his place in Savannah society. For the love of her child, she was involved with every project and served on every committee she could. After dinner with Jack and Kathleen that evening, Teresa wondered if everything she had been doing for the last several years had been in vain. She had planned so many auctions that she could spit, and for what? Money. It was always money. Maybe it was time to start living the life that she wanted instead of being someone she wasn't. But she wondered what that would even look like.

## LOOSE LIPS

The following December, Jack and Kathleen attended the annual candlelight concert at the Cathedral of Saint John the Baptist. As always, it was the most beautiful performance of the year as the St. Vincent's chorus brought the Christmas season alive with joyful hymns. As a prelude to the final hymn, the lights are extinguished, and the crowd is left in complete darkness. Jack pulled her in close and whispered that he had a surprise for her, and she looked over to try and get a glimpse at his facial expression. She finally could see his smile when each side of the Cathedral awakened with candles being lit from one person to another, and the Hallelujah Chorus echoed throughout the majestic walls. The last hymn always gave her chills; this year, even more with Jack sitting beside her. When they walked out of the church, Jack excitedly announced that their ride had arrived.

He took her hand and walked toward a horse and carriage. At least 500 people stood outside the Cathedral, each watching to see who would be riding in the lovely carriage. It was something to see.

Kathleen sheepishly looked around at everyone staring as he led her to the step and said, "After you," and lifted her inside. Suddenly, her embarrassment disappeared, and she was left with only joy. She smiled at Jack as the horses clip-clopped away, weaving through the historic district. An ice-filled bucket of champagne sat inside, and they drank happily and snuggled under a blanket. Although it was only the first weekend in December, all of downtown Savannah was decorated for Christmas. Fresh swags and wreaths were hung at most every home, and gas lanterns and candles glowed brightly at each window.

As the carriage approached Johnson Square, the driver stopped. Jack hopped down and took Kathleen's hand to help her out. He walked her towards the center of the square saying, "This is the square where you stole $10 from me when you parked my truck." Then he got down on one knee and said, "What you didn't know, Kathleen, was that you also stole my heart that day. It has been completely yours since. I know it's only been a short time, but I love you with all my heart. Will you please be my wife?"

Kathleen was so overwhelmed with emotion that when she replied, "YES!" it came out as a scream. An unnoticed drifter, who was napping on one of the park benches, shot to attention and began to yell at the newly engaged couple.

"Woohoo! We're getting married," Jack told the angry stranger who waved him off with an unfriendly hand gesture and turned back to his nap on the bench. They laughed as they made their way back to the carriage.

Christmas was spent telling friends and family about

their engagement, but it wasn't official until his parents had given them an engagement party. Mrs. Murray planned it for New Year's Eve at the Plantation Club at The Landings. The guest list was extremely long and filled with names Kathleen didn't know. The Murrays told her that she could invite twenty people, and she immediately felt sorry for those twenty. The tribe was all home for Christmas break and had a million questions about the upcoming party.

"Is Mrs. Murray as snotty as you make her out to be?"

"How did she tell you to only invite twenty guests without you putting up a fight?"

"Is Mrs. Murray a drinker or a teetotaler?"

All were good questions that she had waved off because she honestly didn't know the answers. Then, during their annual tribe holiday sleepover, when they all wore Christmas PJs, baked cookies, and drank spiked eggnog, they gave Mrs. Murray the nickname "Tyrant." They laughed and laughed, and each took turns barking orders in their best aristocratic voices.

"Ring, ring. I'm hungry. You may serve me now."

"Cheerio, Bootsie. Would you like to go to the club?"

"Beauregard, my good man, can you please go to the loo for me?"

Because of her love for Jack, Kathleen knew she must stop their teasing. His parents couldn't be as horrific as she made them out to be if they had raised such a wonderful son. "Okay, okay. They are not that bad, and his Dad is really nice. I've painted a terrible picture of them."

"Well, even if his Dad is nice, we can't wait to meet T the Tyrant." The name had now stuck, but at least they had shortened it to just T, which didn't sound so horrible.

The night of the party came quickly. It was completely over the top, and Kathleen's friends and family stuck out like a sore thumb, but her parents didn't care at all. They were kind people and were so happy for her and Jack that they didn't seem to notice or didn't acknowledge it if they did.

The tribe was a different story. They had arrived at the party together and were being introduced to Jack's parents when Mrs. Murray suddenly lost interest and started giving orders to the staff. Mr. Murray loved each of them and tried to remember their names, but Jack's mom was completely ignoring them. Finally, Stephanie slung her arm over Mrs. Murray's shoulder saying, "Hey T, let us buy you a drink. Let's head to the bar." The group walked her along to a stool at the bar and quickly placed a drink in her hand.

At first, Mrs. Murray looked angry, but her whole demeanor changed when she started drinking and listening to the girls. Her first name was Teresa, so she thought they were calling her T for Teresa. Then, they started shooing away other people who were trying to get her attention. The girls were wholly engrossed in talking to Mrs. Murray and making sure that the flow of alcohol never stopped. At the hour's end, Mrs. Murray was one of the gals. Alcohol had let her guard down, and she was almost likable.

As Kathleen made her way back to the group, she heard roars of laughter. Mrs. Murray had loose lips when she was under the influence, and she was entertaining the girls with colorful stories about the party guests. As each person passed the bar, she would spill their secrets.

"See that man over there? The heavy-set one with a red hankie in his breast pocket? Well, I happen to know that he wears thong underwear. Roger knows him from the Golf

Club, and the other day after they finished 18 holes, they went to the locker room to change, and Roger said the only thing he saw was butt checks."

"Oh, there's Barb. She once was a B cup, but now she's a double D. If you ever take the boat out to Wassaw Island, take Barb. She has her own personal floatation device."

The roars were becoming progressively louder, but no one outside the group had heard Mrs. Murray. Kathleen realized if the comments continued, they could be harmful. Although she didn't have any warm fuzzy feelings for about 90 percent of the people in the room, it would upset Mrs. Murray the following day.

Kathleen asked Mrs. Murray to accompany her to the powder room and told the tribe to make their way to the outdoor porch to watch the New Year's Eve fireworks. They were stopped by a rotund lady wearing a turban who complained about the young ladies' wardrobes at the party on the way to the restroom. The only young ladies at the party were Kathleen's friends, so it was a personal insult, especially when the woman said, "I guess that's what happens when someone in our position marries below their station."

Mrs. Murray put her heels together, stood up straight to her whole 5 foot 3 inches, and said, "Why Mrs. Sutton, I do recall the first time I laid eyes on you. Mr. Sutton was bragging that he had seen you dancing at the Showboat Adult Club, on the wrong side of Abercorn Street, and had begged you to marry him. I'm quite sure what the young ladies are wearing at this party tonight was much more than what you were once wearing at their age."

"Why I never!" was all Mrs. Sutton could say as she grabbed her husband and purse and made a beeline to the door. It was that moment the Suttons were scratched from the wedding list.

By the end of the evening, Mrs. Murray had sobered up to enjoy the fireworks and still hold her head high in all her desired social circles. Just like that, in one night, she had become one of Kathleen's favorite people.

# SUMMONED

With both college graduation and a wedding on the horizon, Kathleen was stressed. She and Jack had decided on a big cathedral wedding, and it usually took over a year to find an opening on the cathedral's calendar. When there was a cancelation in August, they jumped on the date, even if it was only a few months away. The August heat wasn't perfect, but it was always nice and cool in the church. However, it was rumored that Monsignor was known to play with the thermostat when couples contributions had been slipping, so Kathleen made sure that Jack wrote his checks diligently.

As stressed as Kathleen was, nothing bothered her more than her nightly dreams. In the past month, they had increased in frequency and took on a different feeling. She was still looking for something, but now the scenery was more precise, and there were added gardens, fields, and two massive trees. In her dream, she could feel the breeze blowing and smell the fresh soil from the garden. Somewhere in her search, she would become frantic, almost like she was looking for a lost child, and she would wake with a jolt and her heart pounding out of her chest. She began to dread going to bed each night, and her lack of sleep was worrisome.

One day in early May, as Kathleen was eating breakfast before school, her Mom joined her at the table. She watched as Kathleen tore off a piece of toast and dipped it into the center of her perfectly runny fried egg. Her mother gasped with concern, put her hands around Kathleen's face, and noticed the dark circles around her eyes. Kathleen saw the concern on her mother's face and heard it in her voice, "Tell me, sweetheart, what's going on?" Kathleen burst out crying, telling her about the dream.

"How long has this been going on?" her Mom asked.

"All my life," Kathleen answered, then added, "But it's gotten much more intense."

"Your Dad and his stories of Ireland," she said as she tried to erase the worry from her face and slowly began talking. "Everyone's body reacts differently to stress. Is there something bothering you?"

Kathleen looked down at the table, trying to put her feelings into words. How had she let things get this far? She was so in love that she let her plans change quickly. She didn't even know how to fix them. "I love Jack, Mom. I really do. He's the best thing that has ever happened to me. But, I have never left home or lived on my own. I really haven't even left the South. I wanted to get out of Savannah, but now it looks like I will never be able to do that. I don't want to lose Jack, but I just feel so restless." Tears were running down her face, and her sweet Mom was wiping them as quickly as they fell.

Her Mom offered a solution. "Why don't you take a few weeks after graduation and travel? Your father and I can give you that as a graduation present. You could go to Ireland and trace our ancestors, maybe find out if that dream is real and what you are chasing. It's important to know where you came from before you plan where you're going. When you return, you will not have such a restless soul." Kathleen nodded slowly at first, playing that statement over in her head. But as the reality of what her Mom said started to sink in, her nods quickened. She hugged her Mom fiercely, and they swayed back and forth as the weight of the world was taken off of her shoulders. She knew that this trip felt right, and she couldn't wait to tell Jack.

Jack, however, didn't see the plan the same way she did. One night, after a heated discussion, she told him, "I'm not asking for your permission. I am promising to love you for the rest of my life, and I fully intend to do that. I have never had an apartment or lived on my own, but right here and right now, I am going to Ireland and Italy for six weeks. Our wedding invitations will go out, the cake will be ordered, and when I marry you in August, I will be the best damn wife any man has ever had."

"And what if I say no?" he asked. "You wait until weeks before walking down the aisle to come to this revelation? I don't understand how I should be okay with this like it's no big deal. It's a huge deal to me. I think...," he paused, realizing the weight of what he was about to say, and shakily finished his sentence. "I think you're scared of being with me forever."

Kathleen felt like someone had punched her in the stomach. She was tempted to cancel the trip, but she believed in the sacrament of marriage with all her heart and knew that she couldn't go into it with significant self-doubts. "I love you, Jack. I have no doubts about you. Not even one. But I do have doubts about myself. Do you know that all of the tribe has lived on their own? They all have traveled and lived independent lives. That scares the hell out of me. I can't put all of that on you to give me those things. I need to do this on my own. Please try to understand."

Jack shook his head, "I really don't care what the tribe has done or where they've been. I don't think you realize how amazing you are, whether you've traveled all over God's creation and lived on your own or not. It just doesn't matter." He ran his fingers through his hair. Shaking his head, he said, "I can't believe I'm saying this, but I want you to feel complete when you walk down the aisle and not give me a portion of yourself. I want all of you. But I'm not happy about this, not at all."

She let her fingers intertwine with his. "I love you, Jack."

He pulled her in close and asked, "With all your heart?"

"With all my heart," she answered.

She felt his uncertainty when they kissed, and her heart hurt knowing he doubted her love. But she was sure of her decision and knew that she must do this for herself. Jack was upset, but her friends were much more vocal about her decision.

They were seated in the center of Johnny Harris' beautiful circular dining room with dark wooden booths along the perimeter. The domed ceiling was painted dark blue with tiny lights twinkling like stars. When Kathleen was little, her parents always brought the family to this restaurant for special occasions like First Communion or Confirmation. It could be the middle of the day, but the dining room was perpetually dark as night. She would barely touch her food through lunch because she would crane her neck, staring up at the fake stars.

Her friend's loud chatter carried her back to reality as

they discussed the problem at hand. Kathleen surveyed the room with knowing eyes, searching for familiar faces to make sure eavesdroppers weren't listening to their conversation. Part of Savannah's charm is that in a crowded room, everyone usually knows someone. However, that someone also knows your secrets and isn't afraid to put them on the street.

There had been truth in her Dad's words about true Savannahians always coming home, and she was delighted that The Tribe was back together again. They had been enjoying their time together over the last few weeks, but today was serious; she was in the hot seat.

"I don't understand," Stephanie said. "You are leaving that hunk of a fiancé, weeks before your wedding, to go to a shrine? Am I missing something here?"

Jan interrupted: "I think it sounds wonderful to be on your own, seeing the beauty of Ireland, going to Knock Shrine, and tracing your ancestors."

Agnes piped in, "Well, of course you think it sounds good, Jan. You would wander around the world with your sketchpad and paint rainbows and butterflies, but that's not how Kathleen rolls. We all know that. What's really going on here?"

Seeking courage, Kathleen looked up at the restaurant's pretend night sky, wishing she could tell them about her recurring dream. She knew it was too much to understand, so she told them the partial truth. "I love all of you and appreciate your concern, but I have been feeling this longing for quite some time. When my Mom saw me unraveling and suggested that I take this trip, it was the first time that I felt I was going down the right path. Every one of you has left

Savannah on your own, either traveling or going to school. I haven't, and I need this."

"And Jack is okay with this?" Latrice asked.

"He's not happy, but he understands. Well, kind of. What y'all don't realize is that this isn't about Jack; it's about me. I'm gonna be a much better person because of this. You have to trust me. I know what I'm doing." She pointed up to the starlit ceiling, "It's getting late. We have work to do. Since you all have agreed to be my bridesmaids, you are now my bride tribe, so you need to help me finish planning my wedding."

"Has T given you her guest list yet?" asked Latrice.

"She told me she would keep it under 200 people, but there's no way. She gossips to more than 200 people on a bad day. Bless her heart."

The entire table laughed. Although Kathleen had made significant strides with T, her friends understood what a royal pain in the ass T could be when it came to her precious baby boy. Kathleen had shared with the group that she had decided to say "bless her heart" every time she became angry with her soon-to-be mother-in-law. It was safe to say that Mrs. Murray now had enough blessings to breeze right through the pearly gates and straight into heaven.

For the next hour, the six of them talked about the wedding. Each person left with a small to-do list. With such a diverse group of strong women, she and Jack would have the perfect wedding.

# THE ULTIMATUM

While Kathleen packed the day before her departure for Ireland, her sister Lynn sprawled out on the foot of her bed. She watched as Kathleen placed her clothes into the borrowed suitcase and was bothered by all the practical outfits she was packing. She was a college freshman and had more gentlemen callers than one woman could count.

"Why do you dress like a spinster? You're not even married yet." Lynn trotted off to her room and came back with a handful of trendy dresses and short outfits. Kathleen chose two of the options, happy to jazz up her wardrobe.

"The house is going to be quiet the next couple of weeks without you, but I guess it's getting me ready for your leaving for good," Lynn said. "I'm so happy for you and Jack." They smiled at each other, then Lynn added, "Any of Jack's groomsmen hot?" Kathleen laughed and was grateful for their fun interaction because it took away some of her worries about flying and the upcoming trip.

The tribe had given Kathleen all kinds of travel gear from

their many journeys. They adored Jack but had slowly warmed to the idea of her taking thc pre-wedding trip. They were working hand in hand and making lots of plans with her mom and Mrs. Murray. She was so blessed that her five best friends, along with her younger sister, were her bridesmaids.

The night before the trip, Jack asked Kathleen to dinner at his apartment, and she had been looking forward to it the whole day. Kathleen got to his apartment early and found Jack in the kitchen. He wasn't wearing a shirt and had on workout shorts. "You're early," he said, "and I'm running a little late. I'm just checking on the roast, then I need a quick shower. Wanna join me?"

They had completed the Catholic Pre-Cana marriage Prep in April and had learned about natural family planning. The program was intense and made them both sorry that they weren't coming into their marriage chaste. Jack had suggested that they go to Confession and then wait until after the wedding to have sex. But now that they both knew what they were missing and it had been tough. For that reason, they had forced themselves not to be alone in his apartment.

"Are you serious?" Kathleen asked.

"I wish. And now that I said it out loud, I'm thinking about us in that shower the first weekend I moved into this apartment. I would love for you to get in with me, but I know we promised to wait." He paused for a brief second, hoping she would change her mind, then quickly added, "Heading to the shower, extra cold for me. Be right back."

Her face was hot from embarrassment, so she went to the kitchen and drank a tall glass of ice water. She turned on some music and lit the candles on the table. Jack came out dressed in khaki shorts and a polo shirt. His sandy hair was still wet, and he shook the water onto her before pushing it back with his fingers and walked into the kitchen to finish fixing the meal.

They enjoyed a glass of red wine with deep braised beef and poured another glass as they talked about wedding plans. She wanted to discuss her trip, but he never asked, so she never brought it up. When they finished the wine, he offered her his hand to dance to a slow song. They kissed softly as they swayed to the music and told each other how much they loved one another. As the song ended, Kathleen told him she had to get home to finish packing. That's when all hell broke loose.

"I still can't believe that you're leaving."

"Did you think I would change my mind?"

"Yes, honestly, I did. I thought that once you knew how sad it was making me, you would change your mind. I would never do anything that would make you sad."

"That's funny. You are doing it now."

Shaking his head, he said, "If I'm not enough for you, right here and right now, then I don't see how this will ever work?" Then he looked her in the eyes, almost pleading for her to change her mind.

"Are you giving me an ultimatum, Jack? If I go, then what? We're through?"

Jack silently held her stare for so long that she willed herself not to look away first. Her eyes started watering, so she suddenly turned from him. Mad at both herself and him, she grabbed her purse and simply said, "Goodbye, Jack," in almost a whisper.

Kathleen felt all the blood leave her face as she walked down the three flights of stairs. Her ears began to ring when she stepped onto the ground floor of his Harris Street apartment. She knew that she was about to pass out, so she quickly sat on the last step. She was shocked that he didn't come after her. *Why the hell isn't he coming after me? I don't know what any of this means? Am I a fool? I have to take this trip, something is calling me to Ireland.* She made herself slow her breathing, telling herself that she was doing the right thing. She prayed that it was true.

## GET IN LINE

Early the following day, her Mom drove her to the airport. Kathleen didn't tell anyone that she and Jack had broken up. She had replayed the night over in her mind so many times, wondering if they even did. Her Mom noticed her silence and asked Kathleen if anything was wrong. But she lied and told her she was nervous about flying. She was happy when they started reviewing her itinerary. Kathleen would be traveling for four weeks, working her way from Knock to Dublin, then two weeks in Italy… mainly in Rome. Her parents insisted since she would already be so close, and the flights from Dublin to Rome were so inexpensive that she should visit the Holy See.

The flight was roughly seven-and-a-half hours through the night, so what felt like four in the morning to her was really nine a.m. The final 30 minutes, as the plane made its approach, were the best. She opened the window shade and was too excited to be bothered by the grunts from people still asleep. After traveling across the ocean for the last 3000 miles, she watched as the plane landed. She was waiting to see rolling hills of green, but she only saw various shades ranging from green to brown and assumed they were different crops.

Kathleen was shocked when the plane touched down at the Knock airport. She thought the plane was going through a cloud, but she realized it wasn't a cloud; it was fog. The airport was a single, long strip in the middle of nowhere, a perfect place for a large plane to land. The terminal was built to accommodate the number of pilgrims coming to the shrine and had been opened only a few years.

She walked through the airport and saw historical pictures on the wall. It appeared that a clever and tricky Bishop had found a way to do the impossible: both plan and find funding for the airport. She made a mental note to herself to watch out for those tricky Irishmen.

Kathleen had arranged to rent a small car but soon discovered the rental office was only open on Mondays and Wednesdays, and it was a Thursday. Sile, the lady who operated the rental car agency, also ran a small gift shop in town, so she figured she could try to catch her there. The village of Knock was roughly seven miles from the airport, so she called a taxi. Harry, the taxi driver, picked her up 30 minutes later. He was a funny sort who spoke with a thick brogue. She understood less than half of what he was saying, but his smile made her not care, "Where are you from, and where are you going?" he asked.

"I'm from Savannah, Georgia, and I'm going to stay in a cottage in Knock." She gave Harry the address of the rental and watched his smile disappear. "Hard times have hit th'ome where you are lodging." But as they pulled up, it seemed like anything but hard times; it looked like a street party. It was the middle of the morning, and people everywhere were singing, playing various instruments, and sloshing mugs of ale.

She walked in the front door to complete silence which was almost deafening compared to the party outside. She was in a hallway with a large parlor on the right, and smack dab in the middle of the parlor was a man asleep on a long table. Enough is enough! She stomped into the parlor, but she realized that he was not sleeping; he was laid out DEAD. And that was no table; it was a door. How in God's name was she going to get the hell out of this mess that she called "living on her own?"

She was interrupted by a man snoring in a chair in the corner. *Thank the Lord he's not dead, too*. Running back out the front door, she scanned the premises for someone to ask for directions and noticed two respectable-looking ladies stepping over the men who were sprawled on the lawn. They were both carrying cakes and walking toward the back of the house. She followed them and entered a large kitchen area with at least 50 people sitting around. A heavenly sweet aroma hung in the air, and her nose tried to identify: pastries, breads, and cinnamon. They were happy smells in complete contrast to what she had just witnessed in the front parlor.

A few people sat at a rectangular table, covered with a white lace tablecloth. A handful of people were in line, and when she found the end of the line, she wondered why people join lines, not knowing where they may lead. As the line began to move, she realized that this one had been formed to greet the grieving family. A small man in front announced the names of the people who had come to pay their respects. In turn, they would whisper to him their personal sentiments and be presented to the table.

"Aunt Mary from Galway gives her love."

"The Declan family remembering the plow season of '81."

"Cousins Timothy and Thomas miss their rugby partner."

The line moved quickly, and before Kathleen knew it, she was thrust to the front with no way to turn around. She quietly whispered to the confused announcer before he belted out, "Kathleen from the U.S. wants to know what the hell is going on."

Conversation and eating stopped, and all eyes turned to Kathleen. She looked at the small man with disgust, as though he had just told her most trusted secret to the group. "No! I mean, Yes, I do, but I was just asking this guy upfront. I didn't know he would repeat it."

Confusion hit everyone in the room as they glanced from one to another. Recognition finally hit the older woman sitting at the table, and she said, "Back to your bangers; it's just the Yank letting the cottage." Everyone went back to what they were doing: eating, knitting, and gossiping. The older woman whispered to a dark-haired young man at the end of the table, and he motioned for Kathleen to follow him out the back door.

"Please tell me what is going on. Am I in the right place? Should I call Harry the cabbie back?" But about that time, she saw Harry, the cabbie. He was sitting with a group of men and raised his pint to her. Lordy, that little leprechaun changed hats from driver to partygoer fast!

Looking perturbed by her presence, the man offered an explanation, "My name's Quinn. My parents, well I guess now just me mum, rents the cottage next door. My Da died last Monday, and this is his wake. He will be taken to the church in the morning for burial."

Kathleen looked at him questioningly, "Da?"

"Father," Quinn answered.

"Holy hell!" popped out before she could stop herself. She slapped her hand over her mouth, trying to catch it, but judging by his widened eyes, she hadn't caught it in time. "I'm so, so, so very sorry. Please forgive me. And I'm so sorry about your dad…da."

He nodded only once, then said, "Come along, I'll show ya o'er," and picked up both of her fifty-pound suitcases like they weighed nothing. Kathleen instantly noticed the muscles in his arms, and as she followed behind, she shamelessly looked at how well his tight jeans fit. Even under the weight of Kathleen's luggage, Quinn's height caused him to walk in long strides, and Kathleen had to move quickly to keep up.

On the way over, someone asked Quinn about Kathleen, and he dismissed the man saying, "Just another traveler me mum is renting the cottage to. Sure to be gone before we blink. Go on about yer business," and they nodded at one another.

Quinn glanced at Kathleen, noticing how abrupt he was, and tried to soften his voice. "When an Irish person passes, the family holds a wake. The wake lasts anywhere from two days to two weeks, although it is kept under one week because of the smell in the summer. The body is laid out, and someone sits with it the whole time. Today was Uncle Mike's day, although I hear he's been sleeping off his long night of mourning in a chair in the parlor. On the day of the funeral, all who dwell on the deceased's property escort them to the church and to the burial. There is one last night to celebrate the dead; then it is over."

Kathleen was quiet and listened intently. When death came to her family, there was only sadness, and the grief could be cut with a knife. The idea of celebrating the life of someone who died was refreshing.

Quinn opened the cottage door, set her bags in the foyer, and handed her an old skeleton key. For the first time since they met, she noticed his stormy blue eyes and the sadness that they held. He told her if she needed anything to please come in through the kitchen door. Then he added, "We will leave at 9 o'clock in the morning. No sandals. Wear good walking shoes."

"Wait, what?" but he was gone. Welcome to Ireland, Kathleen.

# BEAUTY AND THE BEAST

Kathleen heard her stomach growling and realized it was only one o'clock in the afternoon in Ireland. Since she wasn't offered any of those yummy sweets next door, she knew she must go find something to eat. She had seen a bicycle propped up outside of the cottage, so she splashed water on her face, pulled her hair into a ponytail, and headed out. She could see the spires of the shrine, so she set off in that direction. She didn't realize that she was riding against the traffic until she hit the first roundabout. She then reminded herself to drive with the traffic flow on the left and enter the roundabout circle on the left. It was confusing, and she was grateful to be riding a bicycle instead of driving a car. She pedaled to the small town and spotted a food mart on the corner. The shop was clean and had both a deli and post office inside. She picked up a basket and went straight to the deli, where two girls about her age were standing behind the counter. One of them welcomed her with a warm smile, "Hiya, would ye like to order a sandwich?" But the other girl never acknowledged Kathleen.

"Yes, please. I'm so hungry I could eat an elephant."

The girl with the smile took her order, "Well, whaddya like?"

"Anything and everything. Turkey?"

"How bout I fix ye something up? I usually can read folks and what they like. I'll make it large enough where all the elephants nearby sleep safely tonight." The soft-spoken girl had a strong spirit and a sweet face. "Me name's Maura, and this is my sister, Leah." She motioned to the other girl who finally made eye contact with Kathleen, offered a curt nod, and walked towards the back of the store. Maura continued, "Grab ya a bag of spuds while ye wait."

Kathleen liked Maura immediately. She tore open the bag of chips and started crunching. "I'm Kathleen. I'm staying at the McMillon cottage up the road."

Maura paused in thought for a brief second, then smiled as she watched Kathleen annihilate the bag of salty goodness. "Are you traveling alone, or do ye hav'a husband?"

Maura seemed very interested in Kathleen's relationship status, and Kathleen wondered if it might have something to do with the handsome Irishman, Quinn, who escorted her to the cottage. "I am getting married in a few weeks," Kathleen told Maura, but she wondered to herself, was she getting married in a few weeks?

Maura's whole demeanor changed, and she leaned in further as friends do. "Oh Kathleen, that's so exciting. I'm so vera happy for you. I hope that you enjoy your stay here with us. If you ever need anything, please come find me and drop in to eat again if you like your sandwich."

"It's so nice to meet you, Maura. I sure will."

Kathleen picked up a few staples for her 10-day stay. She paid and was grateful her parents had helped her convert money before leaving the States.

Kathleen sat down on a bright yellow bench as she exited the store and decided to wait to eat her sandwich when she got back to the cottage. She looked around to find her bearings and took a deep breath. What was that smell? Clean air? On her second deep breath in, she closed her eyes and enjoyed the moment. She felt someone sit down beside her, and when she opened her eyes, she was not alone. One of the largest animals she had ever seen was sitting on the bench beside her. She gasped out loud. "What the hell?"

That got the animal's attention, and its ears stood straight up. Was this a dog or a wild beast? Judging from the animal's size, it could drag her into the woods — never to be seen again. She looked around to see if anyone else was freaking out, but everyone was strolling by going about their business. Then the beast licked her face and laid its head right on her lap. Inside she was screaming "HELP!" but she tried to stay calm. "It" could tear her apart if he wanted to, so she stayed as still as a statue. They sat like that for more than ten minutes, then "it" lifted its head, jumped down onto the sidewalk, and stood next to her bike, waiting. Again, she looked around and saw no reaction from anyone.

She put her bag in the bicycle basket and started pedaling back to the cottage. "It" trotted alongside her like they were one in motion. "This is the strangest thing ever," she thought, and as she turned into the cottage's driveway, she saw that all the people still on the front lawn had gone completely quiet. Someone had called the family outside, and everyone ran to watch the two of them come up the driveway. She parked the bike, and "it" stood beside her.

Mrs. McMillon walked up with the strangest look on her face and muttered, "How? Where?"

Once again, Kathleen was caught entirely off guard and said, "I'm so sorry. Did I do something wrong again?"

"No, child. This was Barry's dog, Wolf. The night of his passing, the animal disappeared. We have been searching for him high and low for days. We have been worried sick and assumed he just died when Barry did. You have brought home a piece of my husband, and I am most grateful."

Mrs. McMillon wrapped Kathleen in an embrace that felt as familiar as her mom's hugs and made her wonder if moms all over the world hugged the same. Then her shopping bags were handed to Quinn to be put in the cottage, and she was led to the big rectangular table.

For the next two hours straight, Kathleen ate and drank. When she finally stood up to find the restroom, she was lightheaded. How many of those pints had she drunk? She touched her fingertips to her temples and stumbled her way from the table. Quinn was suddenly at her side holding her elbow, and she thought to herself that no one had ever led her by holding her elbow. It was such a protective and stabilizing move. Instead of the ladies' room, he led her straight out the back door and over to the cottage.

"Between jet-lag and strong ale, ye need to get some sleep. Off to bed with ye!" he said.

"I am engaged," she blurted out. "Well, I was engaged. I really don't know now."

"Aye?" he said with a flirtatious grin. "Thank ye for telling me." And he shut the door as he left.

"Why did I just say that? I'm a ninny, is what I am. Day one of my adventure is now in the books," she muttered as she staggered across the old stone floor and tumbled right into the best night of sleep she ever had.

# IRISH WAYS

Kathleen shot straight up in bed, trying to remember where she was. The room was so dark that her eyes were having a hard time focusing. As she slowly collected her thoughts and recalled the quaint little cottage in Ireland, she wondered what had woken her up, realizing it hadn't been the dream. In fact, she hadn't had the dream again since the day she decided to come to Ireland. She smiled, hoping that it would never return. Stumbling to the window, she sat on its deep ledge and peered out. That's when she heard the rooster's wake-up call and realized he had succeeded. She had heard stories of roosters waking up everyone on the farm, but actually hearing a rooster was another story. She sat comfortably and watched the tiniest sliver of the sun rise over the fields, growing larger by the second. The next time she heard the rooster, she was grateful it had woken her and was thankful for those early morning moments.

Quinn had told her to be ready at 9 o'clock. Kathleen had

not planned on attending a funeral and wondered what she would wear. She had packed for a summer vacation and brought only two dresses that Lynn had added to her wardrobe, but neither were black. One was canary yellow, and the other was light blue but strapless. He also said no sandals, but the only shoes she had packed were sandals and tennis shoes.

At five-til-nine, she walked out of the door. The entire family was assembled in the drive. They were all wearing the obvious black or brown, but the not-so-obvious summer fabric...wool. Each one stared, looking confused and amused, at her bright yellow cotton dress and stark white Tretorns. Quinn acknowledged her with a nod and motioned her to a place in the pack. Mrs. McMillon greeted her, gave her the once over, and giggled, saying "Yank" under her breath as she kissed her cheek.

The procession began at 9 o'clock sharp with the pine casket carried by Quinn and five other men. All of the family and friends followed closely behind. She recognized Harry, the cabbie, Maura, the nice sandwich gal, and many of the people that had been at the wake. She drifted somewhere towards the middle of the procession. Wolf joined her when they began moving and was close at her side. Quinn looked back, shook his head, and grinned. They slowly wound through the small streets as many friends and neighbors waited for them to pass and then joined in behind the group. By the time the high steeple of the Shrine of Knock came into view, there was an endless line of people behind the family.

Kathleen did her best not to show excitement as they passed through the church's gates. She had no idea that the first time she visited would be while attending a funeral for a complete stranger. She was surprised that the shrine itself was an enormous building that sat entirely separate from the small parish church where the funeral Mass was being held. Wondering how all attendees would fit inside, she was thankful to be in the front of the procession.

The church was cozy, and she immediately felt at home. That's one of the many beauties of being inside a Catholic church – it can be anywhere in the world but still feels like home. A glassed-in chapel, on the backside of the parish church, held life-size marble replicas from the apparition. Across a large concrete courtyard was the shrine, with its stark white steeple that could be seen from most places in town. She would come back later to visit the apparition site and the shrine.

Both the funeral Mass and the burial lasted under an hour, and before Kathleen knew it, she was back in the large kitchen with three times as much food as the previous day. People were everywhere. Ten funeral-goers, sitting at the dining room table, overlooked the fact that a dead man had just laid on it a few hours before.

Music and singing continued until sundown, and people began to trickle out. Kathleen had learned her lesson the day before and only drank two of the dark ales. Designating herself as the cleaning crew, she spent the better part of two hours covering food and putting it away. Finally, her constant yawning got the better of her. She made a quick Irish exit out the kitchen door, determined not to interrupt any of the McMillons or partygoers with goodbyes. As she reached her cottage, she glanced over at the main house and noticed Quinn watching her get safely inside. He raised his hand as if to say good night.

SHE AWOKE Saturday and saw a car in front of the cottage with a note under the windshield.

*You're a fine lady to bring Wolf home to the McMillon's. Keys are in the driver's seat.*
*Will settle with ye later.*
*Sile*

IT WAS A SMALL CAR, but it didn't look old. She remembered to get in on the right but then laughed out loud. She had planned to drive on the wrong side of the road, but as she sat down, she noticed both the stick shift and clutch were on her left. *There's no way I can change gears with my left hand! I'm going to need coffee to get through this,* she thought and jumped on the bike to head to town with Wolf, of course, at her side. Today he seemed to lead her off the main street to a mouth-watering aroma coming from a building with a lot of local foot traffic, so she went inside. She was shocked to see that Wolf had walked in behind her but even more shocked that the waitress and cook acknowledged him by name as he sprawled out in front of a large empty fireplace.

The temperature hadn't made it to 70 since she had arrived, and she wished they would light that fireplace. She now understood why all of the women were dressed in wool the day before. Wool seemed to be the fabric of Ireland. Back home, everyone melted all summer long in 90 to 100 degrees heat. The cool weather was a welcome change.

She sat at a table facing the door and saw Quinn walk in. He looked around the room, but every table was full. She could tell that he really didn't want to sit with her, but his options were limited. She lifted her hand and waved at him to walk over to her table.

"Would you like some company.... other than Wolf, that is?" he asked.

"I would love the company," Kathleen said. "I come from a large family, and even though I love my peace and quiet, I always hate eating alone in public." After placing their orders, they quietly sipped coffee until she broke the silence. "Do you not like outsiders, or is it just me?"

He looked surprised by her question and took a moment before he spoke. "I don't dislike anyone; I just know who to depend on and don't waste much time on anyone else." Then he thought about what he had just said and added, "That sounds like I don't like outsiders, doesn't it?" She nodded, and he laughed. "I don't think anyone has ever pointed that out to me before. Forgive me." He noticed the crinkle between her beautiful green eyes as she listened to him intently and grinned. "I'm sure you're a great person, but when you leave, I'll never see you again. I know that sounds cynical, but I've noticed the trend since my family started renting my old Granny's cottage. How long will you be in Ireland, anyway?"

"Well, I've got a week and a half here in Knock, two weeks making my way to Dublin, and finally, I will finish my trip with two weeks in Italy. But I think I'm in a bit of trouble."

He sat up and leaned in like she was going to reveal a big secret. He raised his eyebrows and asked in a whisper, "What sort of trouble?"

"Oh, no. Not serious trouble. It's just that some joker went and put the stick shift and the clutch on the wrong side of the car. It took me three months to learn to drive a stick at home. I'm not sure my brain will adapt in time to see all of Ireland."

His genuine smile could light up a room. It was a shame that he seldom showed it, and she suddenly wished that she could see it again. He said, "Oh, that's an easy fix. I'm busy this afternoon helping my brother at the farm, but first thing in the morning, I'll teach you how to drive."

"Tomorrow is Sunday, and I need to go to Mass first," she said.

"I don't have the same need as you, but tell ye what, I'll escort you to Mass tomorrow at the shrine. I might need to go and talk to Jesus before riding in the car with ye anyways."

Their Irish breakfast was brought to the table: eggs, scrambled and poached, pork sausage, blood sausage, spuds, beans, mushrooms, broiled tomatoes, brown bread, and fresh butter. She looked at the plate and then at Quinn and said, "I love Ireland."

After breakfast, she opted for a bike ride, but she saw that it was pouring as she walked to the door. Everyone else walked quickly into the rain, tossing on a coat and lifting their collars, but she stood frozen. People passed her while she stood in the doorway, waiting for the rain to ease. Wolf still lay sleeping by the fireplace, and she was surprised by how much she missed him at her side. Suddenly, an older gentleman ran into her as he walked toward the door and held it open for her.

"Whatcha waiting on, Missy?" he asked.

"Well, I was just gonna let the rain slack up a bit," she answered.

He looked at her with amusement. "Waiting on the rain to slow in Ireland is like waiting for an apology; it seldom happens." He nudged her out the door and went about his business.

Kathleen was drenched in less than five seconds, but she didn't care as much once she was wet. She rode into town, bought a raincoat with a hood, a wool sweater, and a couple of postcards, then headed back to the cottage. After peeling off her clothes, she took a long hot shower, fixed a cup of tea, and crawled up on the deep window seat to write notes to both her family and the tribe.

Whenever any of the tribe traveled, they always sent postcards to the others. They would put something different on each card and share them with the group at the next lunch. When the girls got together, everyone would pass around the postcards to get a good glimpse of their friend's trip. Kathleen was so excited that she finally got the chance to write her own postcards.

She sent a nasty postcard to Latrice, who had just started a job with the Savannah Trade Commissioner. Her office was at the courthouse, and Kathleen knew Latrice would be embarrassed when she received it. The postcard had a picture of an almost naked man in a leprechaun hat and said, "Chasing the Leprechaun in Ireland. Sure hope I catch him." Kathleen mailed a historical one to Stephanie. It had different plows that had been used through the years. She selected a religious one for Maggie. It was a picture of the shrine and its brief history, and she hoped the card would remind Maggie to go to Mass that upcoming Sunday since she wasn't in town to call. Agnes got a drinking one with the word "Slainte" on a photo of a Hurling team with its members hoisting mugs. Her choice for Jan was an artsy one that featured a painting of a countryside cottage with a thatched roof. Each postcard was unique and special, just like Kathleen's friends.

She held up the postcard she had purchased for Jack that showed a cute couple snuggling under an umbrella while the rain fell around them. It read, "Having a great time. Wish you were here." She stared at it for a long time until her insecurities took over. *What if I mailed this to him, and he thought we had broken up? I would look like a fool,* she thought. So she decided not to send that one and tucked it inside her travel notebook.

She planned her day trips for the next week and highlighted the routes she would be driving, then enjoyed the sandwich that Maura had made for her on the first day. Maura had been right; she did have a gift of knowing what people liked. Kathleen looked forward to seeing her again soon.

When Kathleen walked out of the cottage the following morning, Quinn was waiting by the car. "Keys?" he said, and she dug them from her purse and tossed them to him. He seemed surprised and fumbled, trying to catch them. Laughing at himself, he got in, pulled the seat position all the way back to fit his long legs, and drove the short distance to Main Street. While walking to the shrine, they passed several small gift shops, each selling rosaries, and statues from the sidewalk. She wanted to stop at each of them, but Mass would be starting in a few minutes. As they hurried through the square, she noticed pilgrims who were saying the rosary at different locations. Tour guides, holding signs, led their groups around the crowds of people. When she approached the apparition site, which once had a rock wall, the hairs on her arms stood up. During the apparition, three figures were said to be floating about two feet off of the ground. The Blessed Mother was the central figure, Saint Joseph stood to her right, and Saint John the Evangelist was to her left. To the left of St. John, and higher up was a full-sized altar on which a lamb faced forward. The figures showed movement but never uttered a sound for two hours. Although it was raining, the figures and the ground under them were completely dry. A marble replica of the apparition with a plaque beside it read:

*On August 21 at about 8:00 p.m, 20 villagers witnessed the apparition of Our Lady of Knock.*

Mass was beautiful and really hit home. The homily was about being men and women of character and living out faith through hardships. After Mass, she asked Quinn if they could go to confession. He declined but encouraged her to do so. There must have been 15 priests hearing confessions, and Kathleen found her place in line with the others seeking forgiveness. What a wonderful attribute of Knock.

When they left, Quinn was quiet and definitely had something on his mind. She felt certain he was thinking about his father and was about to ask him when he said, "Time for a late lunch then a driving lesson."

As they walked into the deli, Kathleen said, "Hi Maura, I'll have my usual."

Maura answered, "Coming at ya, Kathleen."

Quinn looked back and forth between the two women, laughed, and said to Kathleen, "You are a funny little lass, for sure." They ordered to-go sandwiches, and Quinn gave his full attention to Maura as she made them. Kathleen wandered around the store to not eavesdrop. As she drifted around, she realized it was more of a one-stop general store because she saw everything from castor oil to motor oil. Once Maura finished making the sandwiches and Quinn finished his conversation with her, the two said their good-byes and drove out of town.

# THE DRIVING LESSON

The driving lesson began after the already narrow road turned into a smaller one. Quinn pulled over and told Kathleen it was time she became an Irish driver. She wearily climbed into the driver's seat, and the car started perfectly, coming off the clutch in first gear, but stalled when she was switching to second. The next time around, she held down the clutch until she was positive she had dropped it into gear. Driving a straight road was fine, but turning corners was confusing because she automatically went to the wrong side of the road. It was challenging to turn wide when taking a right and hard to hang close when turning left. Kathleen's American brain couldn't make the transition fast enough. A rock wall ran down both sides of the road, and a sheep herd was spotted along the path. The road itself was barely as wide as the car. She thought it was impossible for two vehicles to pass one another but was proven wrong when another car headed towards them. Quinn explained that everyone made room for each other, directing her to a small open space that might have been a driveway, and the fellow driver passed without a glance. They came upon a homemade-looking wooden sign that read "Derry Lough," but Kathleen didn't know what it meant like so many of the road signs in Ireland. Unfortunately, she didn't realize it was the name of a lake until she was upon it. She panicked, and instead of slamming the brake pedal, she gunned the accelerator. They were going straight into the water. Quinn pulled the emergency brake, and the car stalled with only the front tires barely underwater.

"You sure know how to make an entrance, don't ya now?" Quinn said.

Several fishermen wanted to throttle Kathleen for scaring the fish and shook their fists in the air. As she got out of the car, she waved like she was the queen. Irish obscenities filled the air, and Quinn fell to the ground laughing.

They sat in the shade of a large birch tree, pulled out Maura's sandwiches, and Quinn started talking. "I've lived in Knock my whole life, and I've only been to the shrine once. That was in '79 when Pope John Paul II came. I've lived my whole life saying I was Catholic but never questioned it until my da died. Yeah, we are Catholic, but we never go to church or even pray like we did when I was a lad. When we were planning the funeral, I asked me mum if we would have a service at the church. She looked shocked and confused and simply said, 'Of course.' My parents fell away from the church for various reasons, but really more than that, they fell away from everything. We weren't raised with faith. After Mass today, while waiting for you at confession, I thought that when I die, I don't want people to wonder if they would take me to the church for my burial service. Thousands of pilgrims come from all over the world every day to see the shrine, and I don't take the time to walk down the street. How weird is that?"

Kathleen nodded but sat quietly as he talked. He'd known her just a couple of days and was baring his soul. Did he not have friends to talk to? Or was it just easier telling a stranger the things he didn't want anyone else to know? When he finished, she said, "Since I've been in Knock, I've seen an outpouring of respect and love that everyone in town had for the life of your father. He must have been a great man. I don't know why your family stopped going to Mass, but God hits us when we are ready to listen. Maybe it's time to start listening." Quinn gave a thought-filled nod, then focused his full attention on eating his mouthwatering sandwich.

Looking across the lake and past the upset fishermen, she thought of her parents. She had never considered the blessing they had given her by taking her to church and being so vocal about their faith. She never worried if her parents would have a church ceremony. It's incredible how much is taken for granted. She would thank them as soon as she got home. Then she wondered if she would ever have a family? And if she did, would it still include Jack. Her stomach lurched in response.

When she lifted her head, she noticed Quinn staring at her and realized she had been lost in her thoughts. They both smiled, and she couldn't help but wonder what was on the mind of this not-so-wee Irishman.

She drove home from the lake and made no mistakes in doing so, which was a miracle in itself. Feeling brave, she thought that she might be ready to head out on her own. "So, did I pass?" she asked Quinn.

"I don't know what it takes for a Yank to pass a driver's test, but as your instructor, I would advise stayin away from lakes. Other than that, the rolling hills of Èire await you, sweet Kathleen. *N-éirí an bóthar leat,* as we say in Knock. May the road succeed with you!"

"Thank you, Quinn. I had a really nice day."

"So did I," he answered and was almost surprised by the truth of it. This girl wasn't like others. He felt a slight tug on his heart and began to wonder about the story behind Kathleen Kenny from Savannah.

When she walked into the cottage that afternoon, she noticed a basket filled with bread and pastries, along with a note.

*Kathleen,*

*Thank you for everything that you have done for our family. It's lovely to have another female around, don't you know? Please stop in at any time for a cuppa.*

*Sara McMillon*

She opened the basket and began pulling out its contents. She was familiar with many items such as shortbread, ginger snaps, and scones. Still, there were a couple of other things that she had never seen before, like a cake with lemon filling and large loaves of warm bread.

For the next few minutes, she happily enjoyed a taste of all of Mrs. McMillon's treats. She decided that every mouthful was better than the last. She noticed herself humming, which always was a good sign. When she was a little girl, her parents said they could always tell when she was happy because she hummed. As she grew older, she realized the humming happened less and less often. Still, it resurfaced when she was eating something yummy.

Mrs. McMillon certainly had spent quite a penny buying the cute package of sweets. Kathleen wasn't aware there was a bakery in town, but she definitely would need to find out where the treats came from. Her watch read 7:00, so she decided to thank Mrs. McMillon, who was in the kitchen with music playing. She didn't appear to be the same woman that Kathleen had met just a few days before. She was glowing. Not literally, but she seemed to be unusually happy, which seemed uncharacteristic of someone who had just buried her husband.

Kathleen cleared her throat to let Mrs. McMillon know she was standing in her kitchen. As Mrs. McMillon turned to the sound, she smiled and gave her a huge hug. Once again, Kathleen was reminded of how much she missed a loving embrace, and the constant hugs doled out in her family. Guests were always welcomed into their homes with both a hug and a cocktail. She later found out that the cocktail was a Savannah thing, but it was very endearing.

"I wanted to come and thank you for all of my yummy treats. I have been in the cottage savoring the taste of each one," Kathleen said.

Mrs. McMillon smiled big, took her hand, and led her to the table. "Tell me, how were they?"

"Oh my gosh! You have to give me the name of the bakery. I will be going there every morning."

Motioning to her kitchen, she said, "Why it's straight from my kitchen, don't ya know? I'm so happy you enjoyed them."

"Enjoyed them? I devoured them and want more," Kathleen said, only half kidding.

"Well, I once was a baker, and I realized today how much I missed it. Long before I was Mrs. McMillon, I was really something. More than one man was courting me in County Mayo. They took a liking to both my scones and my small waistline. But the one that caught me, over time, let both my baking and my waistline become unimportant. It's not his fault, really. Every person changes, and they lose their passion. But somehow, I let the life I wanted pass me by. I became a farmer's wife and a mother. But now there's no farmer, and there are no babes that need tending." She took a sip of her tea. "I see so much of myself in you. Watching you take outta here on that bike has made me realize that I'm the one that has been holding myself back."

Mrs. McMillon had seemed so strong and intimidating at their first meeting. She was the family matriarch and wore the hat well. But the more they talked, Kathleen realized just how lonely she was. It wasn't the loneliness of someone who had lost a person they love, but the loneliness of living without anyone knowing the real you.

"What about you, Kathleen? Where is your passion?"

Kathleen sat for a long time, playing the words over in her mind, "Where's my passion? Where's my passion?" and she started to get scared. "For a very long time, I thought that my passion was to be able to stand on my own two feet. I worked hard in school to get a good job and just finished college last month. I was supposed to get married this coming August, but I got scared that I wouldn't get the chance to stand on my own two feet once I was married. That is why I came on this trip to Ireland."

"Supposed to get married in August?" Mrs. McMillon asked.

Kathleen focused on a spot on the hardwood floor and

felt her eyes starting to burn. "He said that he should be enough for me, and he loves me just the way I am. Then he told me not to go, and here I am. So, I guess it might be over?" she asked out loud.

"Oh dear," Mrs. Mcmillon said as she quickly put another scone in front of Kathleen and busied herself pouring a glass of milk. She sat back down, took Kathleen's hands and said, "Being independent is a wonderful feeling, but having the love of a good man is a vera beautiful thing, my sweet child. I know in my heart you will figure it all out."

Kathleen noticed their hands were intertwined, and Mrs. McMillon began to pat them. "Now, Quinny said that you took him to Mass with ya today."

Kathleen giggled at the nickname his Mom had used. "Yes, ma'am. We went to the shrine."

"Mind if I go with you th'next time?" she asked.

"I would love that. I checked the morning Mass schedule when I was there today. I am planning to go in the mornings before I go about my day. Quinn said that I need to pray before trying to drive in this country. Would you like to go with me tomorrow?" Kathleen asked.

Mrs. McMillon began to wring her hands nervously. "Oh, so soon? I thought you would be going on Sunday. Well, yes. I would like to go."

The following morning, Mrs. McMillon met her out front. She had an old bicycle with a front basket larger than Kathleen's. She seemed nervous and darted her eyes around as if someone might be watching.

"It's been a vera, vera long time since I have left this house for Mass short of a funeral or wedding," she said as she pushed off and took the lead down the driveway. They rode in silence until they pulled into the church parking lot. Kathleen watched as Mrs. McMillon pulled out a small kerchief veil and positioned it on her head as she walked into the church. She dipped her fingers in the holy water font, walked towards the front, genuflected, entered a pew, and kneeled to pray. She looked up and nodded.

Kathleen smiled and thought, *Once a Catholic, always a Catholic. Old habits from childhood never die.* A few years back, she had gone on a date to the movies. She had walked down the aisle of the theater and genuflected before going into the row. She didn't even realize she had done it until her date had pointed it out. Her heart understood that she genuflects when going into church out of reverence for the Blessed Sacrament present there in the Tabernacle. Still, her brain sometimes went into auto-drive, just like Mrs. McMillon.

After Mass, Mrs. McMillon looked peaceful. As they left the church, Kathleen noticed it was raining outside. This time, she was prepared and grinned to herself as she casually slipped into her jacket and pulled up the hood. They pedaled in the downpour back to the house, hung their coats, and enjoyed coffee, tea, and the yummiest pastries ever. Thus began their new morning schedule, and Kathleen looked forward to their time together.

# THE LOCAL HANGOUT

Off the beaten path of Main Street in Knock was a little bar called Dowling's, where the locals gathered each evening to talk about their day and catch up with town gossip. Kathleen began going in the evenings and making small talk with the bartender. Dowling's always offered a couple of items on the dinner menu, but her favorite was the Guinness Beef Stew. After a couple of nights, she noticed the same faces and began listening to their stories. For the most part, people want someone to tell their stories to, but small-town folks demand it. One of the advantages of not staying in a big city or lodging in a different little town every night was getting to know the residents.

She ran into Quinn on Wednesday afternoon at Dowling's. Although they both were living on the same property, he was gone before she woke each day, so they didn't have a chance to see each other. "How are you keeping?"

"I'm well, and I've been using my mad driving skills to see many places."

"Oh yeah?" he teased, "like where?"

"Kylemore Abbey Castle." Quinn nodded his head, impressed that she had driven so far, so she told him about her day. "I thought it would be an easy trip because it was only 90 kilometers away. But Ireland and almost every other country in the world are on the metric system. It had completely thrown me at first, but I had remembered the conversion formula from good ole Catholic middle school: multiply the kilometers by .6 to convert to miles. Thankfully, my trip was only about 55 miles away. I thought it would take about an hour and a half each way, but I didn't consider the small roads and the paper map that I had to consult at every intersection. The trip ended up taking more than 3 hours one way, so I didn't arrive until mid-afternoon. The Abbey is so beautiful, and I took my time meandering around the gardens until I ran into a scary nun in the cemetery."

"Why would you have gone to the cemetery? Do tell."

"I was taking pictures of all of the Celtic Crosses around the property, and they led me into a cemetery. I kept taking more because the crosses were all different, but then my camera zoomed in on a little old nun praying on one of the moss-covered benches. I pulled my camera away from my eye at the same time she looked up, so I walked toward her. She lifted her sad eyes to me as I approached and reached out for me to take her hand, which I did and sat next to her. We sat in silence for a long time while she focused on a grave with new dirt. It stood out because all of the other ones were much older. Eventually, she dropped my hand and stood to leave, but before she walked away, she said, "The Celtic Curse is a blessing, indeed. It means you're lucky enough to be born with true Irish blood." I watched as she carefully walked down the stone path and then heard the nuns singing 6 o'clock Vespers in the chapel. I made my way to the car as sundown quickly changed to pitch-black dark. The tiny roads, with their blind curves and no street lights, made me realize that even if I could drive alone in Ireland, I probably shouldn't drive alone in Ireland. I think I'm a fairly brave woman, but being alone at night in no man's land scared the hell out of me."

Her voice started quivering, so she paused for a second. Quinn reached across the table and took her hand into his, so she finished telling about that night. "Long story short, I got lost. I accidentally went the wrong way and drove all the way to Newport. I finally made myself pull off at a B&B that still had its lights on. I rented a room from an older lady who was awake watching the telly and was escorted to one of the rooms in her three-bedroom home. The lady was nice enough, but I had to listen to the woman's husband snore all night long. I left as soon as the sun came up and stopped at a small store that was just opening its doors for the day. After getting detailed directions, I drove straight back to Knock. I don't think I'll be driving off by myself again."

Quinn listened to Kathleen's every word and was surprised by the feeling of wanting to protect her. "I'm sorry that you were scared. That's not something you should have to deal with on holiday. What are you going to do now if you can't see everything that you wanted?"

"I might see about taking buses and trains," she said. "I haven't really thought it through yet. But there are a few things that I can see nearby." Quinn nodded, so she continued, "Last night, here in Dowling's, an older gentleman asked me why I was in Knock. He asked if I was tracing my ancestors, so I told him everything I knew about them. He explained that 'my people,' my distant relatives from my dad's side, came from this area, but only one of them remains. The rest either died out or, like my great-grandfather, ventured away from Ireland for a better life. Tomorrow, I'm finding my one last relative." In saying that, she realized she was grinning and also realized that she was still holding Quinn's hand. She slowly pulled it from under his.

He smiled and held up his pint for a toast. "To your people!" he said. They clinked glasses and slowly drank their pints. Two men sitting in the corner eating stew opened cases, which held a guitar and the other a flute. They started playing as if they were sitting at a kitchen table. There was no stage or a microphone; it was just simple fellowship.

Kathleen sat with Quinn for a long time, listening to the music, in the bar that felt like someone's home. The plaster walls were painted yellow. The ceiling was painted green, and shelves held various items: vases, bottles, candles, and sports trophies. Mirrors hung on the walls along with several family pictures, small lamps were scattered about, and the tables all had mismatched chairs. It was a warm and welcoming place, and she hadn't even noticed until that moment. She couldn't think of one bar in the states where she would feel this welcomed. Finally, Quinn broke the silence and said, "Where are you off to next, that is, if you can figure out transportation?"

"I planned to go to the beach and do a little hiking on Friday. Keem Bay and Ballycroy Park."

"Want some company? I've decided to take Friday off," he said.

"I would love some, but only if it's not out of pity. I know you're busy."

"Living on a farm, it takes my family every day, sunup to

sundown, to get the job done. It doesn't leave much time for sightseeing. But right now seems to be a good time to go. What are your plans for your last week in Knock?" he asked.

"As you know, I planned to leave Knock on Monday. I would be on the move for the next couple of weeks through Ireland, staying in hostels and small hotels and seeing as much as I can. I have a long list. But my heart has pulled me in a different direction. I really like the cottage, Knock, and the people I have gotten to know. I decided to continue my day trips and stay here for a couple of more weeks. Your mom said the cottage was open."

"Me mum has taken quite a liking to ye and acts like a schoolgirl around you. I've never really seen her this way."

"I love your mom. She is an amazing woman."

"She's always just been me mum. It's weird to see her biking around town. Yesterday I saw her bike sitting outside of this very bar. She's acting quite odd. People might start talking."

"Well, let them talk. Everyone heals differently and what's important right now is that she's healing."

"I guess so. It's just that she seems so . . ." he stuttered, not wanting to continue but knowing he must, "so much happier now that my da is gone. Whew! I can't believe I said that out loud, but it's been killing me."

"So, you're not worried about others gossiping? You're worried about your mum being too happy?"

"Well, yes. And, no. It's just confusing. I always thought she was happy before. But now it's like seeing her for the first time and seeing her not as just my mum. I can't explain it. But, she's just . . . carefree."

"I think you need to have this conversation with your

mom and be completely honest with her. You might be surprised at what you'll find."

Their conversation had made her homesick. She missed her family terribly, but most of all, she missed Jack. When she finally made it back to the cottage, she called him. It was midnight in Ireland, so it was 7:00 p.m. in Savannah. After four rings, a female picked up, and Kathleen froze.

"Hello," the voice said in a sweet southern drawl. "Hello?" she asked, waiting for a response before hanging up.

Kathleen held tightly to the phone. *Oh my gosh, Jack has someone at his apartment.* She couldn't think straight and continued to hold on to the phone for dear life. *Why didn't I say anything? Why didn't I ask for him? Why am I torturing myself?*

She grabbed the heavy wool throw off the end of the bed and wandered over to her new favorite place; the deep window sill. Looking up at the moon and the many stars in the clear night sky, she thought about sitting beneath a copied version at Johnny Harris with her friends. She cried and cried, finally understanding the meaning of the word homesick. Then she remembered what one of her favorite priests from Savannah would always say, "All will be well, All will be very well!" and had to believe that was true.

# KIN FOLK

At one time, a good many Kennys lived in County Mayo, and their family tree had more branches than Kathleen cared to climb. She had located birth certificates, marriage certificates, and a few death certificates of her relatives. She also discovered one living relative, Brian Kenny, whose farm was right outside of town. That Thursday, as she drove out to meet him, she replayed the story that her dad would tell them every year about Knock.

HE WOULD ALWAYS BEGIN the same way, talking in an almost whisper to get their attention. The children would quiet down and lean in to hear better. Slowly, he told the hardships of the people in Ireland in the 1800s. Then he would pull out the journal. He had an old ribbon that marked the spot. Reverently, he would open the book and begin reading.

. . .

*"AUGUST 21, 1879*

*Everyone in the house was scrambling, quickly lacing up their shoes and looking for something to keep dry from the lashing rain. My mother was yelling the word "Queen," and the only Queen I knew about was Queen Victoria. I was worried why she might be in my small town of Knock.*

*My father had hitched the horse to the cart and already was down the drive. I was 16 and a strong runner, so I caught up to them quickly before they turned onto the main road leading into town. The cart was slippery, so when I jumped onto the bed, I lost my holding. My brother, Patrick, grabbed my coat and pulled me in. Thank God for Patrick.*

*The rain pelted my face, making it sting all over, so I tried to keep my head down. But as we got closer to the old Parish Church, I saw a glow in the sky and squinted my eyes, trying to get a better look. I had never seen such a bright light and couldn't think of anything that would make such a glow. I was so scared. When my father stopped in the clearing, I began to run towards the illuminated area. I turned the corner towards the church's back wall and stopped. My eyes focused on the glowing figures, but they suddenly disappeared, leaving the crowd in complete darkness. I felt the tingling on the back of my neck, and my hands started to shake. I knew that I had seen the Blessed Virgin Mary and also knew that I would never be the same again.*

*I fell to my knees praying, "God, watch over our family. As long as there is a descendent with Kenny blood running through their veins, the story of this night in Knock will be told!"*

KATHLEEN SHOOK off the cold sensation making its way up her spine. Could this really be the same road that the cart had traveled? She was deep in thought when she was stopped by a crossing of cows. She waved at an older gentleman wearing overalls and wellies walking beside them. Still, the cows had continued to mosey by with not a care in the world. Just like when waiting for a train, she had started looking for the caboose. Sure enough, at the back of the pack was a young man wearing overalls without a shirt.

"Hello, handsome Irishman," she said to herself. He looked like a model from the cover of a romance novel, taking his time, walking with a purpose, and slowly wiping the sweat from his brow. He noticed her car, made eye contact, and walked up to the window. Without saying a word, he leaned onto her car and gazed into her eyes. No one had ever surveyed her like that before, and she blushed. Yes, completely blushed. He had more maleness about him than she'd ever seen.

She started talking nervously, "I'm Kathleen. I'm from the U.S., and I'm looking for some of my ancestors. Your cows are really pretty. I'm looking to find you, no sorry, find the Kenny farm. Do you know where it is?" Crap, she wondered what she had just said.

He pointed down the road and to the left, nodded, and walked away without uttering a word. She realized she was sweating; her upper lip was literally framed with beads of sweat. That had never happened to her before, either. It wasn't that he was just gorgeous; even though he was, it was his presence. Almost primal. Whew! She wished she had a picture of him to send to the tribe. They would be on the next plane.

Kathleen drove down the road, turned into the next driveway, and slammed on the brakes. She felt the strange prickle on the back of her neck – the same one that she had each morning when she awoke from her dream. *How can this be?* She scanned the property. Right in front of her was a scene she knew by heart, the place that kept her up many nights. She remembered the long stacked stone fence, the field and the small brook running down the side. Then she noticed the house that sat close to the road. The house was the only thing that had not been in her dream, and suddenly she wondered why. She was so shocked she could hardly move. *This is why I came to Ireland. I have to get answers,* she thought. Although she was scared to death, she also was curious and walked toward the house.

She knocked lightly on the front door, but no one answered. She pounded a little harder, but still, no one answered. The last time she banged with her fist and gasped as the door flew open. A little man grabbed her wrist and yanked her inside saying, "Magpies are in me front. Don't want their eyes upon me. Not ready to meet me maker just yet. Come in quickly and shut the door."

She didn't realize she had been holding her breath until she exhaled into the face of a small, red-bearded man. He was well under five feet tall and looked exactly like every picture she had ever seen of a leprechaun. He had a round face and pale blue eyes that seemed to shine; no, sparkle. She didn't even worry that a strange man just jerked her into his house. She had been so surprised, she couldn't wait to get answers.

"Well, speak up, Lassie," he said.

"Uh, hi, I'm Kathleen, from the U.S. My dad is a Kenny, and I'm looking for Mr. Kenny, who lives here. Would that be you?"

"Well, no one else would be answering me door, don't ya know?" he answered.

"What's with the magpie and yanking me inside?" she asked.

"The magpie are flying all over the front yard today. I'm not ready for me death, so I didn't want them seeing me at the front door. I only use me back door. Don't get many people a callin."

"Oh! Magpie is a bird? I thought it was a pie."

He started laughing harder and harder and said, "Baking a blackbird pie, now that wouldn't be tasty at all. Just like the nursery rhyme." He began singing.

"Sing a song of sixpence
A pocketful of rye
Four and twenty blackbirds
Baked in a pie."

He began laughing again. This conversation was going nowhere fast, but he was so cute she couldn't interrupt him, and eventually, she began to giggle, too.

"Me name's Brian Kenny. Come on back."

He walked her through a pretty house that gave the appearance that someone had once loved it. All of the furniture showed that a woman had decorated and taken care of it, but it looked as if she had walked out of it 50 years ago and never looked back. Everything was covered in dust.

On the way to the back, they passed a formal parlor. On one side of the main hallway was a staircase that led to the second floor. Continuing down the hall, she saw a dining room and finally the kitchen. He then walked to a closed-door behind the kitchen, opened it, and entered into what appeared to be a small cottage inside the house. A fire was going with a smell she didn't recognize, definitely not wood.

A small iron stove of sorts had something cooking in a pot on top. The room also held a kitchen table with two chairs, a cozy-looking rocking chair with another chair beside it, and a bed in the corner with a small dog napping on it. She didn't notice a television, but books were everywhere. A rounded door led to the outside. If she hadn't walked all the way through the house, Kathleen would have thought she was in the middle of the woods somewhere. The whole place was the size of her bedroom at home and held all the necessities that Brian required in this world. He motioned her to the chair beside his rocker.

"Tell me, Kathleen, whatcha lookin for?" he asked as he placed a small unlit pipe in his mouth.

"I'm going to be married; well at least I think I'm getting married. My mother said I should know where I came from before I know where I'm going. So, I'm finding out where I came from. I spent the better part of my day researching the Kenny family. There sure were a lot of you . . . us. Anyway, that's how I found you."

Brian sucked on the pipe, which began to gurgle, and she pictured the spittle being bounced around inside. He continued talking with the pipe hanging from his lips and said, "Ye mum sounds like a smart lady. Tell me what you know and what you found?"

"Harry Kenny, my great-grandfather, lived here in Knock, where Our Lady appeared in 1879. His cousin was an eyewitness to the apparition. Harry had many siblings growing up and not enough food to go around, so he emigrated from Ireland to New York City with that same cousin 12 years later. They lived and worked in the city and remained strong in their faith. Harry's fourth son, my grandfather, moved from New York to Savannah when he was 17.

Your grandfather and Harry were brothers, or maybe half-brothers by a second wife after the first wife passed, but they were brothers just the same. So, I guess that makes you my uncle. Well kind-of," she finished.

He smiled as she unraveled all of her diggings, then said, "Follow me, I want to show you something."

They went out through the rounded back door and down a little stone path that led to a small cemetery. She kept noticing the glimmering lights around the property and reminded herself to ask him about them. The cemetery was marked off with a much shorter limestone wall. He led her through, and they looked at the headstones. Many of the people's names that she had found were lying in this plot of land. As they moved along, he told stories about the relatives, especially the ones he had personally known, but also those before his time. She had been lost in another time and didn't realize it was getting late until the sun began to set.

"We better be going before it's too dark to see," he said. "If ye fall in a graveyard, you'll be in it within the year. We don't want that now, do we?"

"We most certainly do not," she smiled and followed him out. He didn't lead her towards the house but to her car.

"How's about coming to suppa one night?" he asked.

"I would love to. I'm going to be gone tomorrow, but would Saturday work?"

"Saturday it is," he said. "And you are welcome to bring a friend. It was very nice to meet you, Kathleen Kenny. Now, be off with ye."

As she pulled away, she took one more glance in her rearview mirror of the property that had been haunting many of her dreams, and once again, she noticed the flickering lights.

# DAY TRIP

On Friday morning after Mass, Kathleen and Mrs. McMillon rode their bikes up the drive where Quinn was waiting. He was wearing cut-off jeans, hiking boots, and a giant hat.

"Well, don't you look the part?" Kathleen said.

His mom laughed, "I haven't seen ya in that bonnet since you were a wee lad. It suits ya for a day at the beach."

"The sun shines double on us Irishmen. Unless ye want me laid up with sun blisters, the floppy hat is me best friend." Sometimes he laid on the Irish accent thick to make her laugh.

Mrs. McMillon offered food from her kitchen for a picnic. She had put out a basket for them, and they filled it with cold baked chicken from the previous night, thick slices of brown bread, fresh butter, cheese, and blueberries.

They made the drive to Keem Bay in under two hours, hiked a bit, then headed to the beach for a late lunch. It wasn't at all like going to the beach at Tybee. In Ireland, people were just lying in the sand, fully clothed. A few children were splashing in the water, but there were no floats and no lifeguards.

She and Quinn plopped down on a towel and ate lunch. Food always tasted so much better on the beach, and she devoured every last bite. She had worn her suit under her hiking clothes but now realized how foolish it was. She actually wished that Quinn would offer his jacket.

"Do ye get to the beach often?" he asked.

"Yes, but it's very different."

"Sand? Ocean? What's different?"

"I usually have a folding beach chair that I lay my towel on. I spray my hair with Sun-In, rub baby oil mixed with iodine all over my body, and layout while I listen to the radio."

"That doesn't sound very fun. It sounds like a lot of work. How do you hear the ocean over a radio?"

"It's not work at all; it's laying out," she answered.

"Laying out to bake? Why?"

"Well, to get some sun." As she said that, she remembered the complexion of every Irish person she had met – pale and freckled. They tried to get away from the sun, not lay themselves out in it. Then, she laughed too. "I guess we just do things differently."

Kathleen was determined to put her feet in the ocean before they left and coerced Quinn into walking in with her. She was expecting it to be cold, not freezing, and her toes numbed almost immediately. She screamed like a schoolgirl, lost her step, and reached out to him for balance. Her hand went to his muscled arm, and he immediately flexed it, either to show off or offer assistance. She looked at him, smiling down at her, and completely forgot about the chilly water. He steadied her by holding onto her waist, and his eyes never left hers. She broke his gaze when she looked down into the water, trying to get her footing, and he gradually let go.

As they made their way back to Knock, they each would catch quick glances at one another as they fell into comfortable conversation. "Tell me about your day yesterday," he said. "Did you find your relatives?"

She grinned and sat up in her seat excitedly, "Oh yeah! I met Brian Kenny and learned about *my people*."

"You met old Briar, huh? They call him that because he's so prickly and hard to be around, just like briars. Did you go to his place? Was his son, Gray, around?"

"Brian was so sweet. Shame on you for talking bad about my kin. I never met anyone else while I was there. We talked and talked, and then he asked me to come for dinner tomorrow night."

Quinn was visibly disturbed. "You most certainly won't. I hope that you told him no."

"Are you kidding me? I can't wait to go back. He's a bit peculiar and very superstitious, but I really enjoyed being there."

"His son lives with him, and he's pure evil. He has fathered more babies in County Mayo than a whole brigade of men. You wouldn't be safe around him."

"Then you'll just have to come with me. Brian said that I could bring a guest."

"I'll definitely be going with you. I will also need to approve of what you wear. Maybe chainmail?" She laughed and rolled her eyes.

As the sun slowly fell into the evening along the small roads, she realized how completely content she was. The outdoors always gave her a feeling of peace. She was watching the color change in the sky and enjoying the quiet tranquility when Quinn asked, "So, where are you off to next?" She leaned down and pulled out her travel notebook to tell him her next destination when the postcard she had bought for Jack fell out. She tried to hide it, but Quinn yanked it from her hand and said, "What's this, a love letter?" He had swerved slightly off the road while teasing her. After noticing the postcard was blank, he handed it back.

"It's none of your business, and please keep your eyes on the road." Then she thought that he might as well know her story. "Okay, if you must know. I was to be married at the end of the summer. I chose to come on this trip instead of staying home before our wedding. He is a wonderful man, and I love him, but I had many doubts about myself." She paused, realizing what she had just said, and added, "I still do. Anyway, I think the wedding might be called off."

"I'm sorry about that, Kathleen."

She didn't want him to pity her, so she made light of him swerving off the road. "It's not your fault that you're a crappy driver."

"No, I'm sorry that I pried."

"I knew what you meant."

They rode in silence for several minutes before Quinn once again broke the silence, "Hey, I've been thinking. Would ye ever let me come on more of your day trips?"

She smiled tentatively and said, "I would love the company, but I know you're busy. Please don't feel sorry for me. I'm good."

"It's not that at all. Well, except for your terrible taste in funeral clothes and your inability to hold your draught." He paused, then continued, "Would ye ever let me come with you to Italy?"

Her look must have indicated NO because he started

talking really fast. "The rest of my life is set for me. My Da ran McMillon Farms with the idea that my older brother, Brody, would take over. Now he is getting married and moving across Ireland in the fall. He actually is moving to a much larger barley farm to take over their family business. I will be running our farm for the rest of my life. I'm grateful and excited to have my own farm, but it's a huge responsibility. We have lots of workers who depend on our crops for their living. All my life, I've been working under my Da. I've never stood on my own. I feel I need this before I take over the farm. My brother is in charge right now, and this will be my only time to leave. Of course, I can go on my own, but why would I do that if you have the perfect trip already planned?"

She listened to him and could relate to his desire to be independent, even if only for a short time. She wanted to say yes but thought about the spark from their interaction at the beach. "Although a whirlwind trip with a sexy Irishman is very, very tempting, I'm afraid my heart just couldn't take it right now."

His face blushed as he ran his hand through his hair, then sheepishly replied, "I'm flattered, really, and would be lying if I said I wasn't attracted to you, but, wait, you really think I'm sexy? Never mind, off-topic. I'm only interested in seeing something other than Knock for a while and maybe get a little peace and quiet. You seem to understand and respect quiet, which is not typical for your sex. I promise to treat you like a sister and be your personal escort through Europe."

"I don't know, Quinn. I'm not sure how that would look. An unmarried man and woman traveling together? What would people think?" After pondering that for a second, she realized that she didn't give two shits what anybody thought. This was her trip.

He didn't sense her change of mind and kept trying to prove his point, "I can drive and split the cost of everything with you. The car, gas, and food."

She looked out the window and thought for another minute. This arrangement could work since she was worried about being in the big cities alone and was determined not to drive anymore. She was also blowing through her money pretty quickly. Splitting expenses would help tremendously.

"Quinn, you have yourself a deal." She fake spit in her hand and extended it.

He smiled, shook his head, and extended his hand saying, "Yank."

# INVITATION TO SUPPA

Quinn knocked on her door early the following morning with a handwritten message from his Mum.

*A gal by the name of Stephanie called at 2 a.m. I asked if she was dying or if any of your family were dying. When she said NO, I told her if she called that late again that she would be dying. Vera sorry for my touch of temper, She asked for you to ring her back.*

Quinn watched Kathleen read the note and noticed how she was smiling down at it. "Is that from your beau?"

She thought about the woman's voice answering Jack's phone. "No, I don't believe I have a beau anymore." Then she placed the note inside her purse.

"Oh, I'm sorry. Hey, while I'm here, why don't you show me your outfit for tonight?"

Kathleen told him that he was being way too weird, and it was none of his business, but the only way to be rid of him was to show him. On the third outfit, he finally gave a halfway thumbs up.

"Don't you have anything plain? Good gosh, woman!"

"I didn't pack my nun's habit. Sorry," she said, thinking about her sister telling her she dressed like a spinster and wondering if Quinn would have approved of Lynn's outfits. She had packed only the two dresses for the trip and already had worn the yellow sundress to Mass several times. She had been constantly cold, so she wore the dress with her new wool sweater most days. It was funny that she would never have worn the same dress twice in Savannah, especially with an oversized ugly sweater over it, but she didn't seem bothered about her style in Ireland.

"The third outfit will have to do but no high heels," Quinn announced like he was a king giving orders and then left, seeming satisfied. She thought about wearing the revealing blue strapless dress and fixing her hair nicely but decided not to mess with him. He and his family had been way too good to her, so she wore the chosen outfit and had on minimal makeup when he picked her up. He told her how thrilled he was going to the old house because he had never been before and started giving her a little background on the Kennys. They lived on that property for as long as he could remember, and Brian was the last of his family and the Kenny clan. His second wife and her son, Gray, had lived with him in the big house. When Gray's mom passed away, Brian moved out of the big house, but Quinn wasn't sure where he had moved. She knew that Brian now lived in the pretend shack in the back but wasn't going to expose that secret.

As they pulled in the drive, Kathleen felt the tingling going up her neck, and she looked around still in amazement that she had located the place from her dreams and led Quinn up the walk. Eager to see Brian again, she knocked on the door and was shocked when it was answered by the sexy cow-crossing guard.

"You," she said and blushed to her core.

"I see ya found yur way. Ole Bri hadn't stopped talkin about ya."

"Wait, you know Gray?" Quinn asked as his eyes darted from her to Gray. Now she understood why the women in town were falling into his bed, and all of the men had branded him evil.

"We've met briefly," she said. "Is Brian around?"

"Ya, in the kitchen," Gray mumbled.

As she walked towards the back of the house, she thought to herself, "Good gosh, that is one good-looking man. I'm going to have to get myself under control, or it's going to be a long night. I just won't look at Gray, and I'll be fine." She was deep in thought and went straight towards the door to Brian's private cottage when someone called to her from the kitchen.

"Hi ya, Kathleen. Welcome." Brian's smile was dazzling, like a toothpaste commercial.

She was shocked to see that Brian had cleaned the old kitchen from top to bottom, had set the lovely dining table, and was cooking something that smelled marvelous. She felt guilty for being caught up in Gray's sex appeal and hadn't noticed how wonderful everything around her was.

"Oh Brian, it all looks amazing. Thank you so much for having us. Do you know Quinn McMillon?"

"Hi ya, Quinny. I haven't seen ya much since you were a wee lad with your Da at Dowling's. God rest his soul. And please meet my son, Gray." She extended her hand in his direction while focusing on a spot on the floor. She was surprised when he took her hand and kissed it. Quinn stepped between the two, breaking Gray's clutch, and rolled his eyes at Kathleen.

Dinner was beautiful. Brian served lamb chops with potatoes and fresh white bread. He sat at the head of the table with Kathleen on one side and Quinn on the other. Gray was seated on her other side, which made it easy not to stare at him. Quinn kept a steady enough glare on him for the both of them.

All through dinner, Gray flirted with her, making comments that only she could hear. She ignored him completely and kept her attention on Brian, entertaining them with his many tales. He had a story about everything, from why the wind blew to the best time to get a haircut. His superstitious nature was totally intriguing.

Brian left the table to fetch dessert and came back carrying an apple cake with custard sauce. Quinn took one bite and froze. "Wait. I've had this exact cake before but can't remember where. It's delicious."

Brian shook his head and laughed, "You ought to remember, lad, it's your mum's. I bought it from Sara this morning, and the bread, too."

"My mum?" he asked.

"Well, of course. I've been buying her baked goods this week at Dowling's. She sets up her table in the mornings. She once was the best baker in all of County Mayo. The whole town is thrilled that her ovens are burning hot again. In fact, her table sells out in about nine minutes. A line is waiting for her when she arrives in the morning," Brian explained.

Quinn looked like he had been punched in the stomach. "That's why her bike had been in front of Dowling's," he muttered. His face revealed the guilt of thinking bad things about his mom. Kathleen knew he needed to see his mom right away, so she told Brian they were heading home.

They all stood and walked to the door. She gave Brian a bear hug, and he hugged her equally as hard. Then Gray came her way with his arms open, but Quinn ran interference and stopped the attempt. When Kathleen told Brian that she would be back, he said that he couldn't wait to visit with her again.

Gray stood in the open doorway and called out to Kathleen as she and Quinn walked down the path, "I'll be seeing you soon, Kathleen." She didn't turn back, but Quinn yelled over his shoulder, "Like hell, you will," and she giggled.

As Quinn started the car, she noticed the sparkling lights once again. "Look!" she shouted.

Quinn looked back and forth. "You scared the shite out of me. What is it that I'm looking for?"

"Those lights," she said, pointing toward the field.

"I don't see whatcha carrying on about, but lights in the sky are always fireflies, especially in the summer," he said.

"They're not in the sky," she replied. But then they were gone. Maybe there was something special to this land...her family's land...the land of Kenny.

Quinn parked the car, waited for Kathleen to walk inside the cottage, then went straight to his kitchen door. He found his mum singing, her face covered with flour, and the sweet aroma of bread wafting from the oven. As many times as he had seen her cooking in this house, he never remembered her baking and definitely never remembered her singing.

She looked up and smiled, "Quinny! Come have a cuppa."

She busied herself making tea and putting together a

plate of pastries before joining him at the kitchen table. Quinn took a bite, "These scones are amazing, Mum!"

"Thank you, me boy. They are made with love."

"Mum, I went with Kathleen tonight to Brian Kenny's home for supper. He had the best bread and an apple cake that was out of this world. He said that you had made it. I felt like an eejit for not knowing."

"Oh, my boy. How could you have known?"

"I saw your bike in front of Dowling's, and I thought you were enjoying yourself in the bar. I thought you didn't care that Da died and you had wiped your hands of him. I know he was a hard man at times, but I also know how much you loved each other. It surprised me to see you were hitting the town. Then, at dinner, Brian told me about you selling your bread and pastries there." He pulled his chair closer and took her hands in his. "I'm so sorry that I thought the worst of you. Can you forgive me?"

She squeezed his hands tightly. "Always. I can always forgive you, always. When your da passed, I was stunned. He was there one minute, then gone th' next. I was scared and thought, 'What am I going to do now?' The day after, I realized that my whole life had been devoted to him. I had no life for myself, and it scared the hell out of me. Then Kathleen came; God bless her. She is so full of life. One day I saw her take off on da's bike, and it was like I was watching myself thirty years ago. I wondered where that person had gone. So I went and found my very old bike, got on it, and I remembered. Before I was a wife and mother, I was a baker. I quit baking like this because you boys devoured everything I made without ever tasting it. No one appreciated my baking, so I eventually quit. When I started baking again, I realized that it not only made other people happy, it made me happy, too. I loved your da, and I would never, ever change the life that we had, but life is short, and I'm going to fill mine with things I love: my faith, you and your brother, and baking."

They hugged hard and long. She was amazing, and he was so proud of her.

"I'm so sorry I didn't appreciate you more as a lad. Tell me, is there anything that you need help with now?"

"Yes, help me get that bike working properly. It rides like the wheels are square, not round. Also, I'm gonna be needing to find me a bigger kitchen." She reached up to the top shelf and pulled down a large jar full of money, and glanced at Quinn sheepishly as his eyes opened big in surprise. She shrugged her shoulders like it was no big deal.

"Looks like we will be needing a bigger kitchen," Quinn said with a smile.

# SERENADE IN GALWAY

When Kathleen met Mrs. McMillon to ride to Mass, she was standing beside a new bike. "Mrs. M.! Look at you with your new wheels," Kathleen exclaimed.

Mrs. McMillon beamed with pride. "Quinny couldn't fix my old bike, so he bought me a new one. I'm a little embarrassed that people will think I'm showing off, but I sure do love it."

"I think you deserve to have a new bike every 30 years," Kathleen said, and Mrs. McMillon nodded.

When they came home after church, Quinn was waiting. He had asked to go on a few of her side trips but only chose the ones that involved fun and not as much history. After living the history, he was ready for the fun.

They were heading to Galway – an hour and a half drive away – and returning on Friday. His mom had packed sandwiches for the ride, and time went by fast. They moved along as she and Quinn talked about their past week.

She told him about a long walk she had taken on a well-beaten path outside of the city. The locals used it to come in and out of town, often taking for granted the beauty of the countryside. Along its path, she had crossed two of the cutest stone bridges that ran over slow-running streams. His mom had also arranged for her to spend the day at a dairy farm; the family who ran it behaved like her family. They joked around with each other while they worked side by side, then ended their day around the kitchen table, enjoying a meal and telling stories. It was a special memory she would never forget. When she got home that afternoon from the farm, Mrs. McMillon told her that Gray had come over. Mrs. McMillon hadn't told Gray that she was away, so as he was waiting for her to return, she put him to work. He helped her carry in bags of flour and other baking supplies. She somehow talked him into helping her carry her products to Dowling's for the day, too. Kathleen thought it was funny while she explained it to Quinn, but Quinn wasn't amused.

"I don't like Gray hanging around at the house. Has he been around anymore?"

"Yes. He showed up first thing on Wednesday, just as I was walking out the door to Mass." She laughed as she continued. "I told him that if he wanted to talk, that he could attend Mass with me, and we could sit down with the priest afterward for him to explain his intentions. I told him that's how we do it in the states. He said that he was too busy and would see me later, but I'm pretty sure that scared him off for good."

Quinn joined in laughing, "I'd love to hear Gray explaining his intentions with any woman to a priest. You sure don't mince words." Then Quinn told her about his busy week working with his brother. They had a lot to discuss about him taking over McMillon Farms, and it made him nervous. He was ready to blow off a bit of steam.

As they drove into the city, the first thing that Kathleen saw was the Galway Cathedral. Its massive green dome was visible as soon as they passed over the River Corrib. They followed the road around until they found their hostel on Nun's Island.

"I thought we were going into a party town, Quinn. Instead, you bring me to an island of religious sisters?"

He laughed. "Ouch. Ye judge me rashly, Lassie. Nun's Island Distillery has been turning out fine Irish whisky for more than a century."

Quinn pulled the car over to a monument sign. As they read, Kathleen announced, "But the distillery got its name from the Poor Clare Sisters' Monastery that was here for hundreds of years before the whiskey. So there!"

"So we are both right," Quinn noted.

"No. Just me," she teased and bumped him with her hip to make him laugh.

She had no idea what to expect when they checked into her first official hostel, but it reminded her of summer camp sleeping quarters, except it was co-ed. The hostel was an old building that had a vast room lined with bunk beds. She laughed out loud when Quinn threw his bag on the top bunk and uttered a crude joke that he liked to be on top.

In the middle of the room was a young man playing the guitar with people sitting on the floor or lying in their beds listening to him. Kathleen's parents never allowed the opposite sex in their bedrooms, so the happy minstrel made her giggle. She and Quinn were met with a round of hellos, but everyone else pretty much kept to themselves. She realized that she would have freaked out if Quinn hadn't been with her.

They decided to sightsee before hitting the pubs. Quinn knew his way around from coming into Galway occasionally from the farm. The excitement in the air in Galway was electric because the town was filled with young people in university. Galway was beautiful with its many waterways and churches. People were everywhere, and she wondered how many locals owned cars. The town had an incredible feel and was decorated with banners and flags. They didn't make it too long before they were lured into one of the many bars blaring live music.

They started the night out on an impromptu pub crawl, but when they got to the fourth bar – The Healthy Hag – things became interesting. As they walked in, they watched as all of the bar patrons erupted in cheers. The band's main singer welcomed them and called Kathleen up to the stage. Although she had liquid courage running through her veins, she looked to Quinn for approval. He nodded, which surprised her a little, so she played along and walked to the front.

The singer explained his intentions, "We are playing a little game, Luv. I told the crowd that the next maiden to come through the door would be the judge for our singing contest. We really weren't expecting such a fair maiden, so we've been vera blessed indeed." She acknowledged him with her best maiden curtsy as he continued. "Whoever wins gets free drinks for the rest of the night and, if you're game, the honor of walking ye home at the end of the evening. What's your name, Luv?"

She replied, "My name's Kathleen," and the crowd clapped

and yelled. They picked up her American accent in just three words.

"Oh, Lads, we have us a fetching yank with us tonight. You better behave, or you'll have to be answering to meself, you will. Welcome Kathleen, we've got a really nice song picked out for ye. This is how it works. We play the music, and each contestant will sing a bit of the song one by one. You give the nod yes or no as they come through. We have five, wait, make that six contestants. Are you ready, Kathleen?"

"NOT YET!" She reached out and took the beer out of his hand. She took a huge gulp and said, "Now I am," and the crowd screamed with laughter. She was so nervous she was shaking, but as the band started playing, she recognized one of her favorite songs, "Come on, Eileen" by Dexys Midnight Runners.

Contestant number one walked up and started singing. He was dancing around her but couldn't keep up with the music. As soon as he finished the first "Toora Loo-Rye-Aye," she immediately gave him the thumbs down. The crowd cheered, and contestant two strolled up.

He wasn't half bad but showed no gumption. He just stood at the microphone and sang but never even tapped his foot. He began the first line of the chorus, "Come on, Eileen, I swear . . . ," and her thumb went down.

Then number three popped up, who was all over her and barely could hold the microphone because of his groping. She was so grossed out that she gave him an immediate thumbs down. The crowd actually booed him, and as he walked off the stage, he blocked her view of the next contestant. As number three passed the mic to number four, he began to sing. She eagerly waited to see the face hidden behind the contestant at the bottom of the stairs. And then he was there, right in front of her: Quinn.

"Come on, Kathleen, I swear, well I mean
At this moment, you mean everything
You in that dress, ah my thoughts, I confess
You are lovely, Ah come on, Kathleen."

He changed the name Eileen to Kathleen, and holy cow, he was terrific. How had she not known he could sing and dance? The crowd had been silent once he started singing, but they all burst out with applause as he finished the chorus. She was both stunned and enthralled. She couldn't take her eyes off of his eyes...which were blazing into hers. She just kept nodding her head yes.

He continued singing the next verse, and the two contestants behind him in line held their hands up in surrender. She and Quinn stood nose to nose, and the room went quiet, waiting to see how the scene would end. They stood there, frozen, looking into each other's eyes but not making a move. It seemed like that moment lasted forever. The crowd started chanting, "Kiss her, kiss her." He smiled, took one step back, took her hand, and kissed it. The crowd yelled boos but were happy because he had been so much fun to watch.

She and Quinn sat in a quiet corner of the bar, enjoying the complimentary drinks he had won. Their elbows rubbed together, but neither of them moved away. She nervously kept going back to that moment in her mind, wondering if she would have kissed him. She didn't back away. Why? And, where did that come from? How could she push that feeling aside? Obviously, he didn't feel the same because he was the one to back off. Thank the Lord for that. But, she felt guilty for thinking about kissing anyone other than Jack.

In the wee hours of the morning, they started walking back to the hostel. "Forgive me, Kathleen, for putting you in an uncomfortable position. When the crowd started to cheer for us to kiss, I knew that I must take a step back. I would have been a coward to follow the cheers of a crowd." They stopped at the foot of the bridge, leading to the hostel, and watched a pair of swans gliding across the water. She knew that the birds mated for life, so she was always fascinated by seeing a pair together. She looked at Quinn, who was deep in thought. He turned to notice her stare and moved in her direction. "When we were in the bar, I wanted to kiss you, but I told myself that I wouldn't overstep my bounds and would ask for your permission first." He ran his finger around her chin line and asked, "May I kiss you, Kathleen?"

Kathleen nodded. Quinn leaned in slowly. His lips only brushed against her mouth for a brief second. He pulled back, looked her in the eyes, and ran both of his hands down onto her shoulders. This time, he pulled her into a deep kiss filled with longing and expectations. She swayed from the intensity and then pulled away. She touched her lips with her fingertips, shook her head, and ran off towards the hostel. She pretended to be asleep when Quinn finally made it back to their room, but she knew that no sleep would come for her that night. He had obviously visited several more bars after her departure and wreaked of scotch and cigar smoke. Why had she said yes to his kiss? And why did she want to kiss him again?

The drive home the following day was unusually quiet. They barely said a word to one another all morning. Still, she knew that they needed to have a conversation about the previous night. Thankfully, Quinn had begun it. "I'm sorry."

"About what?"

"About last night."

"You're sorry you kissed me last night?"

"Hell no, I'd do it again right now. Good gosh, woman. Did you not hear me tossing and turning all night. What I am sorry about is that it scared you."

She gently touched his shoulder as he drove, and he quickly glanced her way as she spoke. "I'm not sure what this is between us, and I admit that there is something, but we both know it can't go anywhere. You have the farm and Ireland and.....," she paused to let the weight of what she was saying pass, then continued, "and I, well, I have a broken heart."

Quinn nodded and let out a loud exhale, but when she turned to look at him, he stuck his tongue out at her, like her brothers did, and smiled when she laughed at him.

# THE LONE HAWTHORNE

Kathleen had stayed an extra week in Knock and planned one last visit with Brian on Saturday before leaving. When she walked out of the cottage that morning, there was another handwritten note from Mrs. McMillon taped to her front door. It read: "Your friend Agnes called before bedtime last night. Please call her."

Wolf was waiting by her car for a pat on the head. She opened the car door, and the sweet dog hopped in. *Looks like you will be my guest on my visit to Brian today,* she said to herself. When they pulled into Brian's driveway, Wolf started whimpering, and when she opened the door to get out, he bolted. He was one weird dog.

She still couldn't believe that Brian's property was the land from her dream, and she was sad that she would be leaving without any answers. She found Brian sitting on a stone bench near the little stream beside his house. He was in full conversation with someone she assumed was down in the stream, but no one was there as she approached. He looked as if he had been caught and glanced around quickly but then explained. "I was just talking to the fairies. They are worried about me and think that I should show you their secrets."

She was completely dumbfounded, wondering how she had missed the fact that Brian was insane. She had accepted his peculiarities as a part of his Irish upbringing. Yes, he was superstitious, and yes, he had created a hermit's cottage inside his house. Still, he had never shown signs of being delusional. She looked up and noticed him staring at her, waiting on a reaction, so she calmly said, "Why don't you explain them to me?"

"I need to show you, Lassie." He stood up and motioned for her to follow. They walked along the side of the stream for a while and then out into a large field. She had not been past the cemetery and was surprised to see how large a piece of property he owned, but she had remembered the sight well. He led her towards a large tree, but he put his arm across her as they approached. She looked down to notice stones placed in a large circle around the tree.

"We Kennys are lucky to have fairies living on our land. For hundreds of years, these fairies have brought us luck. Our land was fertile, and our family grew strong."

Kathleen interrupted him, looking at the open space, "Were there once two trees here?"

He gave her a once over before answering. "Yes, There were two of these trees here, side by side. How'd you know? Have you been dreaming about this place?" She slowly nodded, and he grinned big, blinding her with his bright smile. "My great-grandfather, the one we talked about, didn't believe in fairies. He thought the trees were a nuisance and in the way of our plows. It was quite a battle in the family because although the Kennys are strong Catholics, we still respected the wee folk. When he took down one of those Hawthorns, the Fairy King took him down, and he never was the same. He woke up the following day and couldn't speak; the whole right side of his body didn't work. The doctor said he had a stroke, but we all knew that he had been cursed. He was bedridden for years before he passed.

My grandfather had been distraught by the actions of his father. His mum taught him about respecting the fairies and told many stories about the curses that lasted for 100 years. When the land started to falter, he understood why. So we worked in the small garden, mostly grew herbs, and made healing tinctures and rubs for people with ailments. The fairy folk helped our garden grow by leaving us special mushrooms and other unexplainable items. They have been good to us through the years, and we have respected them. The 100 years is running out fast; we only have nine more to go. This land belongs to a Kenny who will plow it well, but remember the little folk. I am the last Kenny, but now I found you, or really, you found me." He smiled that perfect smile and grabbed her hand. "You dreamed about this place for a reason."

Kathleen stood frozen, deep in thought, wondering how a reasonably sane person actually believed in fairies. And even more so, how could that person be willing to give away his land to someone he had just met? She loved Ireland, but her life was in the states. She wasn't going to drop everything and settle in Ireland, especially not to babysit fictitious irritable fairies. Tinctures and rubs? What's that all about? Didn't these people have doctors? She had a college degree. She wasn't going to pull herbs and live in a hermit cottage.

Brian must have noticed the worried look on her face. He squeezed her hand and continued, "I'm not going anywhere, young Kathleen. The wee brownies haven't even started helping me yet. Ya know they always help the elderly. But when I do go, I will be putting this property in your care. You don't have to do anything to it; just don't sell it. I beg of ye."

"I don't want your land, Brian. I just wanted to get to know you. I'm sure many, many people would love to have this beautiful land and do as you ask."

"Oh yes, but they are only greedy ones, they are. They want to take all the good from the land but are unwilling to love the creatures on it. I won't have it. I won't."

She let him cool down a bit, then tried to move to a more stable topic by asking about the flickering lights that she kept seeing. His smile grew to the size of the Cheshire Cat's grin. "You have seen the glow of fairies, AND you have th'second sight, m'girl. I knew that you were special. Only a few of us in the Kenny bloodline can see the fairies on this land. You probably won't have it fully until you birth a bairn. That's how it works with the lassies. I've lived me whole life on this land, wondering who would watch over the fairies when I'm gone. Now I've got me answer. It's you, Kathleen."

He reached inside his shirt and pulled a silver necklace over his head, letting it ravel into his hand. Looking down at it, he gave it a quick kiss. He placed it into Kathleen's hand and closed her fingers over it for safe keeping. "This is our family's Celtic Cross. It belongs to the heir of the estate, and that is now you. When me mum died...," he quickly made the sign of the cross, "she told me that it was my duty to have an heir to take over this land. Clearly, that didn't happen. I have begun to see her at times, reminding me of my duty. But now my duty is fulfilled. Promise me that you will stand by your word."

Kathleen was deep in thought and didn't say a word, so Brian asked her again. "Please! Promise me, Lass."

The only response she could think to give him was, "Okay." But she wasn't really sure of what she was agreeing to. She looked into her hand. It was an antique Celtic Cross on a long silver chain. Brian gently took it from her hand, and placed it over her head. He clapped his hands and yelled, "Yee Hee!" then kicked up his heels in a quick Irish jig.

As they made their way back to the house, she stepped on what resembled either a piece of glass or a crystal. Brian was walking ahead of her, so she picked it up and put it in her pocket. She called for Wolf, but he was nowhere to be found. Brian said that he wandered out his way sometimes, so she told him to please call if he showed up.

# COMPROMISING SITUATION

As Kathleen lay in bed that night, her mind was racing. She absolutely did not believe in fairies or ghosts. How had Brian convinced her that she was special? Her dreams had been so troublesome, and she had been so caught up in his stories, that her mind got carried away. *I know better,* she thought.

She couldn't sleep. She watched the clock hands move, praying that she would fall asleep, but as the hands turned to 3:00 a.m., she yanked off the covers and angrily got out of bed. She paced the floors for a while then pulled the piece of glass out of the pocket of the pants she had worn the previous day. She stepped outside to see if Mrs. McMillon was awake and baking but was disappointed that it was completely dark. She sure could use her advice and would love one of her scones. She started pacing again, then came to a direct stop. *What if Brian is telling the truth? How can I know for sure?*

On a whim, she tore through the kitchen drawers and found a flashlight, snatched up her keys, and headed to the car. She drove to Brian's house, pulled in the drive, and turned off her lights but didn't get out. She was waiting for something but wasn't sure what. If she could spot one of those little lights that she had been seeing, then maybe she would have the nerve to follow it. Her eyes were focused on the fields. There was almost a full moon, so once her eyes adjusted, she could see very well.

She watched and watched and must have dozed off but awoke with a start to a loud howling and screeching sound. She sat up and searched for where the sound was coming from. Suddenly, something slammed into her car. She screamed and fumbled, trying to turn on the car lights, when she saw a man holding a shotgun beating on her window. He stopped and pointed the gun at something in the field. "Don't come any closer, or I'll shoot," he yelled.

She jumped out of the car when she realized the man was yelling at Wolf. When he aimed the gun at the poor dog, she grabbed his arm and pushed it upward, and the weapon exploded into the air. The piercing sound of the blast burst into her ears, and she covered them with her hands in pain. She then examined them, expecting to see blood, and was grateful when she didn't. But the pain and the high-pitch ringing remained.

"What kind of nut job are you?" she screamed. "That's my dog." She walked straight up to Wolf and hugged his neck to calm his cowering and shaking. How in the world could this huge animal be so scared? What had happened? She walked back towards the crazy man to chew him out. He had thrown the gun on the ground and was waving his hands, trying to tell her something. All she could hear was the piercing ringing in her ears.

The man's attention went from her to the house, and he

scrambled to pick up his gun. The front door to Brian's house flew open, and a young, pretty half-dressed blonde stumbled onto the porch and ran down the steps. Gray was running right behind her with only a sheet around him. The car lights caught the gleam of the gold ring on her finger, and Kathleen realized why the man was here in the middle of the night with a gun. He had come to retrieve his wife.

The girl grabbed him and was crying and screaming at him in a voice that Kathleen couldn't understand because of the constant ringing in her ears. The girl was half exposed, and Kathleen was embarrassed to be in the middle of this scene. The man was full of rage as he turned the gun towards Gray, and time seemed to slow. Her hearing had returned enough to hear him. "I swear. It was all her. I pushed her away. She keeps coming to my house and climbing into my bed. I don't love her. She won't leave me alone," he rambled.

The girl ran to her husband and dropped to the ground, clinging to his legs. The man shot at Gray's feet while the young girl cried out hysterically. When the angry husband turned to console her, the police car sped up the drive, and Brian sleepily came down the path from the back of the cottage. The Garda separated the love triangle and settled them in the back of two vehicles. They wrote down Kathleen's information in case they had questions and drove off. Still wearing only a sheet, Gray yelled for Brian to follow them to the station to bail him out.

Brian and Kathleen didn't say a word as they stood shoulder to shoulder and watched the car disappear down the driveway. Brian then turned to Kathleen and meekly asked, "Care for a cuppa?" She nodded and followed with Wolf closely at her side.

Kathleen was shocked when she noticed the clock on the

kitchen wall read 4:30 a.m. A lot had taken place in a short amount of time, and it was still dark outside. Brian poured the two cups of tea and brought them to the table with a small glass bottle of milk and sugar. He sat down heavily and said, "Gray is gonna put me in the grave early. He's got more good looks than he knows what to do with, and those looks are trouble. When I married his mum, God rest her soul; Gray was a wee lad of five. His da had died early, and I wanted him to know a father. I gave him me name and treated him like my flesh and blood. We went to church every Sunday, and he received his sacraments. During his early school years, he would go to confession a good bit, but over time, he stopped going and became selfish. I truly believe that his good looks are a curse, not a blessing. When all eyes are always on you, you think you're special and can do no wrong. The wee folk hide from him. They tell me he is too busy looking at himself to see them, and they seem to be right. He calls me an old fool when I talk about them. In the last year, he has become unsettled, and bad things seem to follow him. This is the third time this month that he has been hauled off to jail. This month, don't ya know? It usually isn't for breaking the law, but he's always in the middle of something not right. If you hadn't been here tonight, he might have been in the grave himself. Had that poor boy found his bride in Gray's bed, instead of in Gray's t-shirt, he might have been wearing a bullet...which is more than what he was actually wearing. The police warned him that they were running him out of town if they found him in any more compromising situations. I think this might be pretty compromising."

Kathleen reached over and held Brian's hand and asked, "Can they really do that?"

"They told me not legally, but they could hold him in the cell for 28 days a month, and they would continue locking him up until he's gone. He tends to drive all the men in County Mayo a bit mad," Brian said with a sigh.

Just at that moment, they heard the front door open, followed by Quinn's voice, "Kathleen? Kathleen? Where are ya, lass?"

"We are in the kitchen. Come on back," she yelled.

Quinn stomped down the hall, rounded the corner like a bull charging, and then stopped dead in his tracks when he saw her and Brian sitting and sipping tea.

Brian just smiled and said, "See what I mean?"

Quinn was embarrassed that he had stormed into Brian's house. He had awoken at 4:30 a.m. when his mum started baking. They had planned to attend Sunday Mass with Kathleen, so he had been confused when her car wasn't in front of the cottage.

"*Where is that girl?*" he thought. "It's *too early for her to be sightseeing*." He had talked briefly with her when she got in yesterday from visiting Brian, and she seemed very preoccupied like something was on her mind. Had Gray finally beaten her down? The thought made him angry, and his hands bunched into tight fists. Was it out of jealousy or concern? They seemed to be blending together. He sat and sipped tea while his mum was baking, but he couldn't settle himself. He had feelings for Kathleen, but he most certainly didn't love her. Not yet, anyway. So what was this? Friendship? His da had told him that a male and female could never be friends because the man always would want to have sex. He thought back to Galway and shook his head. They definitely had chemistry, and he hoped to find out where that could lead. Hell, maybe his da was right.

Quinn watched the clock constantly, and finally, at 6:15, his brain got the best of him. He would ride out to the Kenny farm, and if her car wasn't there, he would come home and wait. He was sure she wouldn't miss Mass...she never did.

As he pulled in Brian's drive, Quinn saw her car. "Damn him to hell!" he said about Gray. He was going to give him the beating that he deserved and didn't even knock at the door. He walked right in the front and called her name out loud as he headed for the stairs to the bedrooms. That's when he heard Kathleen's voice answering from the kitchen. Were they already up for the day having breakfast after a long night? He stomped down the hall and came to a screeching halt at the sight of Kathleen sitting with Brian. He was sure that his face showed everything. Kathleen looked surprised at his angry face, and he was ashamed for doubting her.

They said their goodbyes to Brian, called for Wolf to come, and as they walked to the car, Kathleen said, "So, what brings you out so early in the morning, Quinny?"

"I showed my arse, didn't I?" he said.

"Not exactly. I'm calling it the Gray Effect," she answered.

As they walked to the car, Wolf started whimpering and cowering toward the field.

"What's going on with Wolf? I have never in my life seen him scared of anything," Quinn asked.

She started explaining the events from the night and had come to the part about Wolf running from the field howling when Quinn stopped her immediately. "Wolf was running from the field whimpering, and the crazy guy thought he was attacking him? What was Wolf running from?" he asked.

"I honestly have no idea. Can we go and have a look in the light of day?" They walked towards the field with Wolf following tentatively. They passed the small cemetery and headed down the path towards the large tree. She decided to open up and tell Quinn the story of what brought her to Ireland in the first place – her dreams and the knowledge that the land once held two Hawthorn trees instead of one. She hadn't noticed they had stopped walking until she finished and was surprised by the worried look on his face. They began walking again, and she explained further how Brian had told her that the remaining tree was a fairy tree that must remain undisturbed. He listened and nodded but didn't comment. As they approached, Wolf began to howl, which startled both Kathleen and Quinn. Wolf then began running in circles around the rocks that encircled the tree. Confused, she looked to Quinn, and he seemed almost scared. They both jumped when Brian grabbed their shoulders.

"You need to be going, m'dear Kathleen. Things are amiss. Call Wolf and be on your way." She looked at him worriedly, but he winked and said, "Do as I say, m'dear."

They walked back up the path to their cars, but Quinn looked puzzled. He had a million questions to ask her but kept them to himself. She didn't have the answers she was looking for and realized it would forever remain a mystery. But she now understood enough to concede that the circumstances around this land were nothing that she could explain.

# FAREWELL

Kathleen had never been to a farewell party before, so it was fun to see how many people had turned out to bid her goodbye. She had only been in Knock for a few weeks, but these people had become her friends, and she was going to miss them terribly. Mrs. McMillon had baked an enormous cake, Maura had made trays of sandwiches, and Dowling's had sent pots full of stew. Quinn had brought a notebook that he laid out for everyone to sign. On the front, he had written:

For Kathleen
to remember the people of Knock
and their words to live by

There were some funny ones:

Harry the cabbie – "Irish women are like teabags; they don't know their own strength until they are in hot water."

Sile – "May you live to be a hundred years, with one extra year to repent."

And there were some sweet ones:

Mrs. McMillon – "May you have the hindsight to know where you've been, the foresight to know where you're going, and the insight to know when you've gone too far. Please keep in touch. Love, your mum in Ireland."

Brian – "Your Irish blood is your most priceless heritage. God bless you, sweet Kathleen."

THE NOTEBOOK MAY HAVE BEEN the best present she had ever received. When the musicians in the crowd started unpacking their instruments and playing, everyone was in such great spirits that they all sang and danced to the deafening music. Would she really be able to leave all of these people? How was it that she felt like she belonged in a place so far from home?

One by one, the revelers began to leave. Some walked out on their own, others were helped out because they were too tipsy, and still, others made a quiet Irish exit. Either way, the crowd had dwindled to a few people, and she couldn't find Quinn anywhere. She finally spotted him in the back, talking intimately with Maura. She had wondered if they had feelings for one another but was surprised when she felt a jolt of jealousy. They actually fit nicely together. Maura was sweet and seemed like she would be a perfect farmer's wife. That thought made Kathleen think about Gone with the Wind, and the Ashley, Melanie, Scarlet triangle. *Oh shit, I'm Scarlet,* she thought. *He's not supposed to be with me*. She knew it in her heart, but she still wished she had been the one sitting in the back with him instead of Maura.

As Kathleen scanned the room one last time, she realized that she wasn't the only person whose eyes were on Maura and Quinn. Maura's sister, Leah, was standing near the doorway watching them. Leah's expression surprised Kathleen because it wasn't her usual scowl - it was worry.

When she got back to the cottage that evening, she called home and caught up on things. Her Mom and Jack's Mom had met with the tribe a couple of times for lunch to go over wedding plans. Kathleen didn't have the nerve to tell her mother on the phone that the wedding was off, and hated the thought that all of their hard work was in vain.

At the end of their conversation, her Mom asked her to please call her friends. She said they seemed eager to speak with her, and Kathleen promised that she would. But that promise was postponed by her sleepiness. The following morning they were in a rush to get on the road, so the call was never made.

The drive to Dublin was smooth, but she felt a change in her gut as they neared the city. She was leaving behind the Ireland she had come to love – the small towns and the narrow roads. They were speeding along on a six-lane motorway, and she felt her stomach tighten with knots. She started doing what she usually did when she got nervous: talking non-stop. "Okay, we will be here for two days, and our flight leaves at 6 a.m. on Monday. Sile said that we are to leave the car at the airport car return."

He laughed at the way she pronounced many things, but names were the worst. "How do you say her name again?" he asked.

"Sile like tile," she explained.

"No, no. There is a lot of thought put into naming your babes. Sile is pronounced Shee-la. It is the Irish form of the name Cecilia, the patron saint of music. It is good to name your young ones after a saint. They are our intercessors, so children are taught to ask them for help whenever they have a hard time."

She decided, right then and there, that she would give her children saint names, and she would rely on them often. She vaguely remembered Sister Gilbert telling her in eighth grade that Kathleen came from Catherine. She had tried to choose a confirmation saint and had finally selected Saint Catherine of Sienna. Her quote – "Be who God meant you to be and you will set the world on fire" – was still one of her favorites.

As they continued to drive toward the hotel, she was amazed at the enormity of Dublin. In such a short drive, they had left the quiet countryside and entered the very congested city. After throwing their bags in their fourth-floor hotel room, which was furnished with twin beds, they walked onto the elevator, or what Quinn called the lift, and pushed the down button. When the doors opened on the third floor, they were shoved to the rear by a group of rowdy men.

Kathleen began to look at them one by one, trying not to stare. They all wore ladies' dresses and wigs but had smeared eye-black under their eyes, like football players, and held sports pennants and flags. She looked to Quinn, questioning, but he just shook his head. So she turned to the 6'2" man next to her in the hot pink dress and Cher wig and said, "Nice dress."

The elevator went quiet. He motioned to his one-inch high heel shoes, "I was really worried that my shoes didn't match. What da ya think?"

She gave him the once over and replied, "Well, if I had legs like yours, I would go for two-inch heels, but you sure are pulling it off." The elevator passengers burst into laughter. The man put his arm around her, and she realized the side of her face was directly in his armpit hair. She cringed and wiggled her way out. "I'm buying you a pint. Follow us." He then looked at Quinn for approval, who nodded yes. On the walk over, Quinn whispered in her ear, "Have you coughed up a hairball from Cher yet?" Kathleen swatted him on the arm, and she cringed again.

The bar was right outside the hotel and jammed full of men, screaming and shouting at the television. All the testosterone in the air made it feel electric. The hot-pink-dress guy put a pint of Smithwick's Red in their hands and started explaining, "Alright, you're a Yank. I'm sure your fella knows, but we are here for the games. It's the Five Nations Summer Warm-Up game." She looked confused. "Rugby, lass. The greatest sport of them all."

She nodded in acknowledgment, "So what's with the dress?"

"We are here for Wales. Ireland and Wales are the greatest opponents. They call us Celtic Rivals." He smashed his fist to his chest and let out a loud grunt. Everyone around him then did the same. "Whenever we clash, me and my mates dress up like eejits for a bit of fun. Everyone has a bloody good time, that is, until we get home. We will be chopsing for weeks with our women."

Suddenly, something happened on the television, and everyone went wild with cheers. He turned back to Kathleen and asked if she wanted to sit on his shoulders. "No, I'm good down here, but thanks," she said. "And, thanks for the pint." He nodded and returned to watching the screen.

Quinn looked at her and mouthed, "Chug!" She turned up her beer, then he grabbed her hand and pulled her out onto the streets. "Things could get ugly in there fast, and I would be way outnumbered. It's best if we go about our business."

Before leaving Savannah, Kathleen had made a list of the things she wanted to see in Dublin: Trinity College and the Book of Kells, Saint Patrick's Cathedral, Grafton Street, and the Dublin Castle. They had two days to see it all before their flight to Italy.

Each day, she and Quinn grew closer. It may have been the knowledge that they would never see each other again, or it may have been the time in their lives where they felt independent. Whatever the case, they were drawn to each other. On their final day in Dublin, after crossing the famous bridge at Saint Stephen's Green, Quinn sprawled out in the grass and motioned to her to sit by him. As she did, he gently leaned his head into her lap. The intimacy of the moment worried her, but as she looked down at him, she saw that his eyes were closed as he turned his face up towards the sun. She noticed his strong jawline and the way his lips moved when he talked. They confided in one another, sharing their deepest secrets and dreams. Knowing they would never be repeated. They both wanted similar things...a happy marriage and a family. Still, they accepted that they would never have those things together. They were from different worlds.

That night they ate at Leo Burdock's, where she had the best fish and chips of her life. They ended the evening in the Temple Bar area. She began to notice that the places in the city's center were very tourist-oriented. The bars were fun, and most had bands and signs that read, "Live Authentic

Irish Music." Suddenly, "I'll Tell Me Ma" was rafting into the street with everyone singing the chorus...

"She is handsome, she is pretty
She is the belle of Dublin city
She is courtin' one, two, three
Please won't you tell me, who is she?"

It was a great song, but Kathleen just shook her head in disagreement. She knew in her heart what "Live Authentic Irish Music" meant. It was people you knew by name, sitting around a table enjoying each other's company. The Ireland that she had come to love wasn't a big city, but a beautiful countryside, good food and ale, and the community of County Mayo.

# NO PROMISES

The taxi bulleted down the highway from Rome's Leonardo da Vinci Airport and into the city. The driver maneuvered like all of his fellow Italian motorists, weaving in and out of traffic and using the horn more than he used the brake. Kathleen and Quinn couldn't contain their excitement when they were dropped outside of the two-bedroom flat on Campo di Fiori. They were not only happy to have survived the car ride but also thrilled to see the city.

Rome is set up with numerous piazzas – open public squares – and Campo di Fiori was a favorite. Each morning, it was set up as a fresh market with fruits and nuts, fresh vegetables, loaves of bread, meats and cheeses, alcohol, clothing, and just about anything a person would need in their daily lives. Everything broke down and completely disappeared by midday when the many bistros with their bars and sidewalk seating opened.

After walking through the area and visiting Piazza Novena, the Pantheon, and Trevi Fountain, they returned to home base. Sitting at a little street-side café, Kathleen's entire body was alive with flavors, smells, and the buzz of people. Although Rome was a big city, it felt intimate. The whole time she was in Dublin, she felt the size of the city. It was a melting pot for people from many places, and could have been plopped in any country and been just fine. But Rome had a way of making the bigness blend into the background, and wherever she was at any moment felt very personal.

Kathleen was very aware of Quinn's presence as they sat at a small, four-person table in the cozy cafe. They both leaned towards each other, lost in conversation. After taking a sip of the Amarone wine, she felt the trace of it remaining on her lips. His eyes watched as she licked off the hint of wine, then they slowly traveled up her face. She held his gaze for what seemed like an eternity, feeling the emotion and desire they had. They were both surprised by the restaurant owner when he cleared his throat. "Scuzi, could I move you to a smaller table? You look as if you wouldn't mind being closer, and I could use the space for another table." They both smiled in agreement and were offered free shots of limoncello for their troubles. She drank hers down in one gulp and felt the burn of the sweet liquor quickly moving all the way to her ears. Feeling relaxed all over, she laced her fingers into Quinns and finished her glass of wine.

They left with full bellies, walking hand in hand toward the Tiber River then strolling along its path. As soon as they saw the Vatican, they knew what their destination would be. They walked faster and faster in anticipation and didn't stop until they reached the paving stones that led to Saint Peter's Square center. The golden lights against the black sky made the Basilica, and its adjacent walls, appear almost majestic. They slowly began to spin around, trying to absorb both the enormity from every view. The 140 Saints that sit on the

Colonnades of the square seemed to welcome them as they slowly approached the Basilica itself. She couldn't wait to go back the following day when it was open.

They walked back towards their apartment slowly, taking in their surroundings quietly. Thinking about everything that they had seen that day, Quinn asked, "Is Rome everything you thought it would be?"

Kathleen sighed, "Everything, and more. I can't wait to see more. But… there's one more thing I need to do before going to bed on my first night in Italy."

"Oh yeah?" Quinn asked and wagged his eyebrows at her. "What might that be?"

"GELATO!"

He couldn't believe he had fallen for her comment and shook his head, saying, "Not the same thing I had in mind, but a close second. Lead the way."

They broke up their sightseeing by areas on their first full day. They hoped to see the Vatican and its gardens and meet a Savannah friend – Father Sullivan – a priest teaching at NAC, the North American College for Seminarians.

The line into Saint Peter's Basilica began to form at daybreak, but the doors didn't open until 7 a.m. They picked up a loaf of crusty bread at the market and munched happily while waiting in line. The crowds of people moved slowly through the massive doors and spilled into the most magnificent sight she had ever seen: the Basilica. She and Quinn stopped dead in their tracks and grabbed each other's hands. She didn't realize she was crying until she felt the cool temperature in the church on her wet face. She couldn't remember a time that she had been so full of emotion.

Kathleen and Quinn looked at each nook and cranny inside the Basilica, then walked to the gardens. They had reserved spots on the garden tour, which didn't disappoint. The winding garden path offered a surprise at every turn with breathtaking features and grottos. She could have stayed there for the rest of the day but had to keep up with the quick-moving group.

Borgo Pio was a road right outside the Vatican walls and was lined with Catholic stores and restaurants. They met Father Sullivan at Roberto's – one of his favorite eateries. Although they had not intended to stay for lunch, Roberto had other plans. When Kathleen ordered café au lait, he brought her wine. And when she said she wasn't eating, he brought her Caprese and lasagna, topped off with tiramisu. Roberto ran back and forth from the kitchen and talked to no one, in particular, the entire time. By the end of the meal, they all were giggling. Their conversation was relaxed, and they all seemed to enjoy the afternoon immensely. As they parted, Father Sullivan asked if they wanted to go to Assisi the following day. They were excited about taking a day trip and agreed wholeheartedly.

The next day they boarded the 7:05 a.m. train to Assisi. It was a slow train, making several stops in the countryside along the way. At one point, a lady even stepped onto the train with chickens. Kathleen realized how she was witnessing what goes on in the everyday lives of locals who use trains for transportation. She smiled and thought that she was accomplishing exactly what she had set off to do: broadening her horizons.

From the train station, she could see Assisi high up on a hill. It was a medieval walled city with steep roads, walkways, and paths, and Fr. Sullivan knew his way around well. They were happy to follow. They saw the Basilica of St. Clare, the Basilica of St. Francis, and the monastery for his order, the Franciscans. The streets wound around to beautiful restaurants and shops, and she never stopped wondering what was around each corner.

After lunch and gelato, they wandered onto a hiking path on the city's outskirts. It was as if the holy sites Quinn had seen in the last couple of days had opened his heart and mind. He began profound and religious conversations with Father Sullivan. Kathleen felt almost embarrassed to overhear and was grateful when the two men began to slowly pull back from her, deep in conversation. Always competing to win, Kathleen began to pump it to the top and crossed their pretend finish line without either of them in sight. The prize from the mountaintop was the fantastic view of Umbria. On one side, she looked down over the beautiful stoned city of Assisi with tiny ant-like visitors wandering through the maze. On the other side of the mountain were miles and miles of green fields and hills spotted with an occasional beige stoned house topped with a red clay roof. The sites were spectacular, and she was happy that she got to experience it alone for a short time.

As Father Sullivan finally approached the top, Quinn somehow seemed different. The worry lines across his forehead were gone entirely, and his underlying sorrow seemed to have been lifted.

She jokingly asked, "What happened to you?"

"I went to confession. I made things right, and all of my burdens are gone. When we walked into Saint Peters yesterday, I realized that I had to take a stand. Either I was a Catholic or not, but I couldn't be passive about my faith anymore. Like I told you, I have felt this way since Da's funeral." He motioned all around him, "being outside and seeing the things we have seen. It was time," and an enlightened smile spread across his face. He looked like a completely different man. He fell into a deep peace-filled sleep on the train ride back to Rome while Kathleen and Fr. Sullivan caught up on Savannah news.

After separating from Father Sullivan at Termini station, the two of them came to a decision. To keep their attraction from one another at bay, they would go to their separate rooms when they got in every evening. And so began the perfect plan for the rest of their visit. The next several days were a whirlwind, but since they had broken the city into sections, they were able to dive in hard touring the Colosseum, Roman Forum, Spanish Steps, Castel Sant'Angelo, and the Holy Stairs. They also took a cooking class that they chuckled through with an unamused chef. They went to unhurried dinners and long walks every evening, and she discovered that Rome was everything she thought it would be, and Quinn had been the perfect person to share it with.

On the last night, while walking home from a late dinner, Kathleen bought her parents a nice bottle of wine to thank them for sending her on the trip. They had a short walk back, so Quinn carefully carried it to the apartment for her. "I am so thirsty. Sure would be a shame to waste this good bottle of wine."

"It's not for you; I'm taking it to my parents."

As they came a little closer to the apartment, he continued, "This sure is getting heavy. We should drink it down a bit. Don't you think?"

"Yeah.....not a chance."

When they opened the front door to the flat, he teased one last time. "This is my last night in Italy with my beautiful new friend. Sure would be nice to finish it on the balcony with a nice bottle of wine."

This time she paused before answering. "Okay."

"Really? Wait, I was just kidding around."

"No, you're right. That would be a perfect ending to our trip."

They walked into the kitchen and opened the wine, but Kathleen laughed after searching for wine glasses. "We have to be staying in the only place in Italy that doesn't have wine glasses." Quinn raised the bottle to his lips. "You wouldn't!" Kathleen snapped, but he did. Then he grabbed the kitchen towel, wiped the top, and passed it to her. She shrugged and said, "When in Rome," and took an ample swig.

They carried the bottle to the balcony. Dangling their feet off the side, they looked out over the city. Both were lost in their own thoughts as they passed the bottle back and forth. Each of them was trying to enjoy the present moment while bidding farewell to their relationship. Kathleen tentatively started the conversation. "I honestly can't imagine the rest of my life without you in it, but I think we both know that we must put this summer into the past so that we can embrace our future." Their eyes locked, and she nervously touched the side of his face. She realized her hands were shaking when she asked, "Quinn, may I kiss you?" Just like he had asked her in Galway, but this time she was asking and only had to ask once. He placed his hands over her shaking ones and kissed her deeply, with all of the longings from the past weeks. He scooped her in his arms and carried her to his bed. She had played out in her mind how their story would end, and each time was the same, it would end in bed. She knew in her heart that there was no other way to tell him goodbye, reasoning that her soul would burst from sorrow if she tried.

Afterward, as she laid with her head on Quinn's chest, she was surprised by her emotions. She knew how their bodies would react to each other but was amazed at the compatibility of their lovemaking. However, without the promise of forever, it felt pointless, and she was suddenly embarrassed to be lying next to him. As soon as his breathing slowed, and she was sure that he had fallen asleep, she left his room, went to hers, and locked the door, praying that he would still be asleep when she left at 5 a.m.

QUINN HEARD the door shut and knew that Kathleen had left for the airport. He stumbled into the nearest chair and rested his head in his hands. "Why?" he groaned out loud, "Why am I not a stronger man?" He sat for a long time, lost in his weakness. All his life, he had tried to do the right thing, but when he messed up, there wasn't anyone or anything that held him accountable. Sure, his sins burdened him, but over time he had become numb to them. But the high he had been riding since he went to confession with Fr. Sullivan was offset with a low he had never felt before. He questioned if he were strong enough to live the life of a Christian.

He had a late-night flight, so he tossed his belongings into his oversized backpack and walked around for a few hours before catching a cab to the airport. He needed to clear his head, and fresh air always helped. He walked through Campo di Fiori and down one of its many small streets that led to the Tiber River. The sun beating down his back made him irritable, and the many tourists along the sidewalk added to his aggravation. He ducked into the first air-conditioned public space he came to; the church of San Giovanni Battista dei Fiorentini.

The church was nearly empty, and he welcomed the

much-needed silence. He sat down on one of the many pews and let out a small sigh. He hadn't realized how much he had missed the quiet of Knock until that moment and knew in his heart that it was time to return. He was surprised when his thoughts turned to Maura, but his heart was filled with sorrow. How could he give himself to her when he was so broken? She deserved more.

He glanced around the church, and a glow against a side wall caught his eyes. He walked across the church towards it, totally intrigued, and came upon a small table with something sitting on top. As he crept closer, he was shocked that it was a bronze foot, illuminated by candles and overhead spotlights. It appeared to be glowing. Rome was filled with innumerable relics of Saints, but he was surprised by this one. The marker beside it read, "Foot of Saint Mary Magdalene – The first foot to be entered in the tomb of the risen Christ." At that moment, he remembered his talk with Fr. Sullivan about God's infinite Mercy. If Jesus forgave and loved Mary Magdalene, a sinner, then maybe he could forgive him, too.

He bowed his head for a moment, collected his thoughts, and thanked God for leading him to that spot. He then began searching for a priest to hear his confession.

## THE WEDDING IS ON

Kathleen arrived at the airport extremely early. In her attempt to leave the apartment way before Quinn woke up, Kathleen was at the airport before 6 a.m. After checking in, she needed a cup of coffee. When she opened her purse, she saw the note from Mrs. McMillon asking her to call her friends. Doing the math, she knew that Rome was six hours ahead of Savannah, so it would be midnight in Savannah. She thought to herself which one of her friends would be awake at midnight on a week night, and called Maggie who answered on the first ring and screamed when she heard Kathleen's voice.

"Oh my gosh, oh my gosh! You're alive! Your Mom told us you were fine, but we knew she must be lying. Why haven't you called?"

"Oh, Maggie. It's such a long story. I made a HUGE mistake."

"With Jack giving you an ultimatum and you still going to Ireland? Yeah, we know all about it."

Actually, Kathleen was referring to her night before with

Quinn but was slowly putting the pieces together of what Maggie was saying. "How do you know?" Then, she thought of the only other person who knew. "Jack. Tell me everything….slowly."

"Jan had been trying to get in touch with Jack. She had him on her list to contact about boutonnieres and groom's gifts, but he kept dodging her calls. She left him three messages, both at home and work, but he never called back. Jan told us that he was avoiding her, so we decided to bombard him at home. One night, we picked up two bottles of wine and Chinese food and crashed his apartment.

Jack had been uncomfortable for the first hour, but after a few glasses of wine, he loosened up. Then we pinpointed him on the decisions that needed to be made. When he switched to drinking bourbon, things got interesting. Latrice asked him if you were having fun and he immediately answered that he didn't know, he hadn't talked to you. We all knew it had been almost four weeks, so Latrice started asking questions. You know how she is; relentless. Anyway, he told us the whole story – that he had told you if you go to Ireland that it was over and you went anyway. He put his head down in his hands and we all looked from one to the other nervously, not knowing what to do. Then he asked us if it was really over. Latrice had stood up and raised her voice to him saying, 'And you just let her go? What's wrong with you, man?' Then she asked each of us if we had talked to you since you left, and we hadn't. We tried to get in touch with you but wow, that Mrs. McMillon is a scary little thing. Maggie finally stopped talking, but there was complete silence. "Kathleen? I will tell you this. Jack loves you."

Kathleen sobbed into the phone. "Oh, Maggie. Will you please get in touch with Jack? Tell him that my plane lands at

9:30 tonight and if he wants to see me, I would love for him to be there."

As the plane reached cruising altitude, Kathleen slowly replayed in her mind the events of the prior evening. It was almost as if it had happened to someone else and she was hearing about it. Had it really happened at all? But her heart knew the truth and the anxiety slowly started building until she was in a full blown panic attack. The Lord always knows what He is doing, and He placed an older American woman next to her who assumed she was scared of flying. The woman held her hand gently and told her to breathe, in and out, in and out. Then she asked her what she usually did when she was upset, and Kathleen pulled her rosary beads out of her pocket. The lady smiled and patted Kathleen's arm as her fingers guided her to the peace that she knew was there in those powerful little beads. As soon as she finished, she could think again.

The night before she left for Ireland, Jack had told her that he didn't see how they would work if she took the trip. She had assumed they had broken up, although neither of them had said the words. Then she called and a woman had answered the phone. But Maggie said he loved her, so that really confused her. Were they still together? And if so, did she need to tell Jack about Quinn?

She started to think about Jack and his time alone in Savannah. What if he had assumed they had broken up? What if he had a one night stand? And what if his one night stand lived in another country where he would never see her again? Would I want to know? She answered herself quickly — absolutely not! What good would that do? It would only cause doubt, and she didn't want to ever doubt Jack. She had her answer. She would carry the weight from her weakness alone.

The absurdity of it all was that she didn't doubt, for one second, her love for Jack, or their future. She never had second thoughts or cold feet, but her promiscuity could hurt the one person that meant more to her than anyone else in the world...and he didn't even know about it.

When she walked into the Savannah airport, she felt like a different person and couldn't believe that six weeks had changed her completely. She had always been curious about what kind of person she would be when she wasn't dependent on anyone else and had wondered if she were strong enough, and smart enough, to live on her own. She had been worried that she would fail. But as she hurried toward the baggage claim, she thought to herself, *I'm a badass. I just went to Europe alone.* That small taste of independence gave her a huge confident boost and made her realize there was nothing that she couldn't do, if she set her mind to it. She liked the new person she had become. She had found herself in Ireland, and in knowing that, she would never regret the trip. She also realized that it wasn't only her inward self that had changed, she even looked different. Living for weeks on a farm, and hiking around Europe, had changed her daily routines. She had stopped curling her hair every morning, and instead let it fall freely down her back. She also didn't spend any time on her make-up like she used to, and simply wore powder and mascara. The natural feel was refreshing.

After grabbing both of her heavy suitcases from the luggage belt, and placing their handy little wheels on the floor, she was stunned to see Jack come through the door. Her heart went to her throat and she caught her breath. She watched him scan the room searching for her. When they made eye contact he came to a halt. The change in her appearance must have confused him, and he looked her over and smiled with appreciation. The next change he noticed was much more evident. No longer timid, she didn't wait for him to come to her. She closed the distance between them quickly, dropped her luggage in the middle of the very busy terminal, flew into his arms and kissed him with such force that it nearly knocked him down. As they pulled back, a grin spread across his face, but his eyes were questioning her. She simply said, "With all my heart!"

"I'm so sorry, Kathleen. I love you so much, I just…." He didn't get to finish his sentence because she pulled him back for another kiss.

"Take me to your apartment and show me how much," she replied. This made him give her a questioning look and she answered before he spoke, "We can start over our *waiting until marriage* promise tomorrow, but tonight I want to be with the man I'm marrying in three weeks."

Later that night in Jack's apartment, as they lay entwined with each other, her heart knew. Jack was her home. And with the promise of forever, she felt the excitement of starting their lives together.

# I DO

The next morning she awoke on Ireland time and was waiting on the steps of the Cathedral for the doors to be opened for Mass. As she sat, she did an examination of conscience. She was so downhearted by the mistakes she had made that her stomach began to cramp. She looked around for a place she could wretch if the feeling didn't pass, at the same time that Father McCreedy opened the massive Cathedral doors.

He was accustomed to greeting a few homeless individuals first thing in the morning. They would lay on the cold granite steps to find some respite from the 100 degree heat during the night. But Father McCreedy was surprised to see Kathleen staring at him, like a deer in headlights. He nodded to acknowledge her, so she asked Father if he could hear her confession.

She bared her soul to him for 20 minutes straight. The kind priest listened patiently while offering her several tissues as she cried her way through her confession. She finished with the Act of Contrition and was glad when she choked out the final, "Amen."

She knew that mascara was smeared down her face when she exited the confessional, but nothing could contain the relief she felt having been forgiven of her sins. She walked towards one of the back pews, knelt, and prayed her penance.

Letting her eyes wander around the beautiful church, she narrowed her gaze on the tabernacle. Guilt washed over her once again, trying to pull her into the deep waters of misery. Her eyes fell to the floor as her shoulders sagged.

The sun coming through the triple stained-glass windows behind the alter drew her eyes up, and she refocused on the tabernacle once again. She had been forgiven of her sins, and she trusted in God's mercy. *That part of my life is over. I'm giving it to you, God. I can now give my heart entirely to Jack.* She smiled to herself, nodded, and made the sign of the cross.

WITH ALL THE running around for the wedding, she and Jack barely had time to talk about her trip. At first she thought about Ireland constantly, but after a week or so, she stopped thinking about what time it was in Ireland or how everyone there was doing. She focused on the wedding and Ireland quickly became a separate world, set apart by an ocean and a fading memory.

As the days passed, Kathleen and Jack both were running crazy, but their moms were winning the marathon. They were constantly on the phone with each other, and her mom was forever on her calculator. Final appointments and staying within the budget were her mom's everyday life, but her eyes never left Kathleen. Her mom was concerned when she noticed Kathleen dazing off or sleeping late. Kathleen had been in school for so long, then for the last several weeks she had been on vacation. She was trying to find her new normal, which in Savannah would never be normal. Her mom asked her only once, "Kathleen, are you happy?"

Kathleen assured her with a huge hug and smile by saying, "I am the happiest," and prayed that the comment wouldn't be a segue into the conversation about sex that she had been dodging all week. She found it funny that they had not had the conversation before. Her mom had left her hints including a book on her bedside table about female sexuality and reproduction that looked like it was published the same year as *See Jane Run*. Then, she put a smaller book about the sacrament of marriage sitting on her bathroom counter. Her mom was struggling with how to deal with her eldest daughter. Kathleen should have pointed out to her that when her mom was her age, she was married and had three small children. Finally, Kathleen took the bull by the horns and said, "Hey Mom, thanks for leaving me all the sex books. They were really cool, and I stayed up late reading them every night. Real page turners; I just couldn't put them down."

"Cheeky girl," her Mom said and swatted the top of her head.

The days flew by and suddenly she was standing in the back of the cathedral holding on to her dad's arm for dear life. The main church doors were closed, and it was just the two of them. He kissed her cheek and told her he loved her, then lowered her veil over her face. The enormous wooden cathedral doors flew open, and she could see all the way down to the altar where Jack was standing. Her dad patted her hand for reassurance as the wedding march started to play, and she took her first step down the long marble aisle. Four hundred people wouldn't notice if she tripped coming down this massive aisle, would they? Why did she want a big cathedral wedding with 400 guests?

It had taken her almost 20 minutes to get in her beautiful dress with its scoop neck, tight waist, and 15-foot lace train beaded with tiny pearls. Her heels clanked on the marble floors in time with the count of "Here Comes the Bride." One, two, three, four. One, two, three, four. Keep walking. Could this aisle be any longer? Who came up with wearing a veil over your face? She couldn't see anything. One, two, three, four then BOOM, Jack came into focus and everything suddenly felt perfect.

Cathedral weddings at 7:30 p.m. are always formal, so Kathleen had printed "black tie required" on the invitations. The women wore floor length gowns and the men were in tuxedos. It was such a special occasion; they had hardly received any regrets. The church was built in the 19th century and had endured many hardships: Civil War, hurricanes, fires, and vandalism. Out of all of the churches that she had seen that past summer, she thought her Savannah cathedral was the most spectacular. It was especially so at night, with all of the candles burning bright. Once she and Jack were in the front of that massive church, all of the guests faded away, and it felt as if they were the only two people in the world. Father Sullivan had agreed to officiate while he was home for a few weeks, so the homily was warm and personal. As the ceremony was coming to an end, she presented a small bouquet of blue hydrangeas to the Blessed Mother, praying to her for intercession. The priest gave the final blessing and announced them as Mr. and Mrs. Jack

Murray. While trumpets played they walked out of the church to a round of applause.

The reception was at the nearby DeSoto Hotel, which was decorated with hors d'oeuvres stations, a champagne fountain, and a black checkered dance floor. A distinct line seemed to be drawn between her family's guests and Jack's, but once they were on the dance floor everyone meshed. The only rumble of the whole night was when all of the tribe tried to catch her bouquet. Best friends are the sweetest things ever, but when they each want to be the next one to marry, all niceties fly out the window.

She and Jack stayed as late as the hotel would allow them and kept shaking off their parents' request to leave. Once the last bar was broken down, they finally began their exit into the night. This time Kathleen stepped into the horse and carriage as a married woman. As all of the people they loved most in the world bid them farewell, she knew that she had never been happier.

# THE DYNAMIC DUO

When Kathleen and Jack returned from their honeymoon, they quickly transitioned into the young-married-couple routine. She had started her job with a local accounting firm and they were grateful for her fresh outgoing attitude while working in an all-male environment. However, after only five weeks, Kathleen and Jack had an unexpected surprise. They had decided to embrace Natural Family Planning, and to wait a little while before starting a family, but the results were positive. She was pregnant.

Although it was a shock, she and Jack were beyond happy, and the accounting firm was willing to let her work from home for the first year after delivery. Jack's mom was excited and marveled at how easily Kathleen's body handled a pregnancy compared to the difficulties she once had. She spoiled her with attention, checked on her constantly, and became the person Kathleen leaned on for help. Kathleen and Jack's mothers had become close while planning the wedding, so it was nice to have both matriarchs by her side.

The tribe, however, had their reservations and were trying to accept the idea of one of them having a baby. She was the first of the group to get married and pregnant, and the change in the air was noticeable, mostly because she was the only one not holding a cocktail at lunch. Kathleen explained, "Just think, you guys have a designated driver for months to come. This isn't going to change a thing." But everyone knew that this was the first step to not being carefree. As the months passed with her morning sickness, swollen ankles, and baby showers, the time for idle chit-chat fell further and further away. The responsibilities of motherhood began to hang over her head as visible as the crib mobile from her baby registry.

She and Jack had found a house on Jones Street that needed a little TLC but it would be a perfect place to raise a family. Her plans for redoing her kitchen were quickly replaced with transforming an upstairs room into a nursery. She and Jack gravitated to that room often and sat on the floor lost in the thought of how quickly their life together had taken root. Sometimes she would pinch herself in amazement for having such a beautiful life. Their home's carriage house sat on the back corner of the lot and overlooked the lane. Its downstairs was a garage, and upstairs was a two-bedroom apartment. When Kathleen and Jack bought the house, the realtor explained that long-term renters were already in the apartment, but were surprised to find out that the renters had been there almost as long as the carriage house.

They set up an appointment to meet the tenants the week after they moved into the house. The women who lived there invited them for cocktail hour and were surprised when Kathleen didn't know that cocktail hour was always at 5:00, something that she would never forget again. She had planned ways to help the carriage-house ladies feel like they were a part of her world, but as she stepped onto their porch she soon realized she wanted to be a part of theirs.

As if on cue, the ladies sing-songed their "Come on in" greeting with magical southern drawls. Jack looked scared and she stifled a laugh as they entered. Each of the ladies seemed like a force to be reckoned with, but together they were explosive. Miss May Simpson didn't have a hair out of place and was wearing a dress, heels, and pearls. She was tall, thin, and very put together and said that she had kept the books at the First African Baptist Church for more than 40 years. She was working there when the Rev. Martin Luther King, Jr. came to town, and was a huge part of Savannah's desegregation movement. She moved slowly, but with grace, and her eyes showed how very bright she was.

Miss Marilyn Bouchelle was quite the opposite of Miss Simpson in appearance. She stood about 4'10" on a good day and was wearing capris pants – which she called pedal pushers – an oriental-looking shift top and several cloisonné bracelets. She had a solid white pixie haircut and wore large turquoise ear bobs. She didn't go into as much detail about her past but mentioned taking her toddies to Bonaventure Cemetery once a week to visit her late husband. Most days she was a docent who gave tours at the Telfair Museum.

Although the two ladies were polar opposites, they seemed to fit perfectly together. The ladies offered highballs but when Kathleen pointed out she was seven months pregnant, they said, "Phooey!" and handed her a glass-bottled Coke. Everyone sipped while the ladies showed them around the apartment.

Kathleen and Jack wandered around but stopped in front

of a large picture window facing the lane. Looking out rewarded them an amazing view of the Cathedral's steeple several blocks away. It was the perfect angle, across many lanes and over trees, but there it stood; the place she and Jack became husband and wife. It seemed like yesterday and, at the same time, long ago. Miss May grabbed Kathleen's hand with her free one and escorted her to the couch. "Now tell me, Ms. Sunshine, what's got you so upset?"

Kathleen looked to Jack, who just shrugged, then to Miss Marilyn who nodded in agreement with May. "You look like the weight of the world is on your shoulders, and you with a babe on the way. Worrying is no way to welcome a little one."

Kathleen was completely taken aback and was borderline angry. She contemplated rushing the door and running away, but somehow a deep sigh escaped her mouth. "I'm scared," she said. Jack looked at her, shocked. Kathleen seldom showed her vulnerability. How did this lady get this out of her? Jack sat down beside her, put his arm around her, and hugged her into his chest.

Miss May cooed, "Now see there, ain't nothing to be scared of. You gonna be a great mama and daddy. Look at you both. You just lean on each other. It's okay to be scared."

Suddenly the tears started flowing. Jack hated to see her cry, and always did anything and everything to try to take her sadness away. But he was upset at how quickly her mood changed and had no idea how to help. She cried and cried, until the sobs turned into a laugh, and then everyone was hugging.

They gave her another Coke and a Kleenex, and for the longest time they sat there talking and laughing. At sunset, she and Jack left the carriage house and its occupants, understanding that both were truly special. She felt blessed to have the fabulous female duo enter her life. Jack laughed as they walked across the garden and told Kathleen that he would take care of the main house and she could handle their tenants. Between the tribe, their mothers, and the new ladies in the backyard, Jack was increasingly outnumbered in her world. She prayed that their baby would be a boy to give him some company.

THOMAS WAS BORN two months later and instantly became the center of their lives. Kathleen realized she had much to learn about being a mother and it saddened her that none of her friends could help. She leaned on the elder women in her life: her mom, Jack's mom, Miss May, and Miss Marilyn. They were constantly popping in and out, and she hung onto their every word.

On one of her many visits, Mrs. Murray had shared a story about cardinals. She told Kathleen that cardinals built nests in places where they can hear newborns cry, so Kathleen was pleasantly surprised the first time she noticed them outside of their home. It was an early morning in May, and she was walking the floors with Thomas. He was only weeks old and was an early riser. Some days, she would go out on the back porch and sit on the swing for some fresh air before the heat of the day ran her back inside. She would wave to Miss May and Miss Marilyn as they left for work and they would call out, "Hey darlin, how's our baby boy this morning?" She would nod and reply, "He is amazing. God is good."

She began to notice how much she enjoyed the squeak of the swing and the sun on her face, but she especially loved the cardinals. The birds were attentive to them, and appeared to listen when she gently sang to Thomas as they glided on the swing. Jack had hung a feeder, packed with suet, behind her row of hydrangeas. It appeared to be the most unappetizing brick of food, but the birds flocked to it like bees to honey.

The cardinals were different from the magpies in Ireland. Brian was scared of them, but she was enamored by the cardinal's presence and felt blessed to have them nearby.

# THE CELTIC CURSE

Screams. One of the children was screaming. Kathleen bolted awake and shot out of bed. Being the middle of the night made the sound boom through the house. Her heart was pounding as she ran up the stairs, grasping the handrail for balance as she tried to blink the sleep from her eyes. She followed the wails into Thomas' room and was grateful for his dump truck night light as she ran to his bed. When she was tucking him in the night before, he had said his belly was hurting, and she mentally did a checklist of what he had eaten. He had just turned five and loved having a small scoop of ice cream every night after dinner, but sometimes it didn't agree with him. As she turned the corner to his room, she saw Thomas was writhing in bed screaming. She sat on the side of the bed and tried to calm him by rubbing his head but realized he was burning up with fever. She talked to him softly, hoping to calm him where she could run to the medicine cabinet, but he was inconsolable; screaming and clutching his side.

Kathleen was 36 weeks pregnant and was afraid to carry

him down the stairs, so she yelled for Jack, who was up the stairs in two seconds. His hair stood straight up, and expression was pure worry, as he placed his hand on Thomas' head. He looked at Kathleen and asked, "Why didn't you wake me earlier?"

"I was running before my feet hit the ground. Something's not right, we've got to get Thomas to the hospital."

Jack stood frozen. When someone he loved was in pain, he was paralyzed with fear. Kathleen touched his shoulder, and calmly said, "Thomas is sick. I'm sure it's nothing, but we need to find out by getting him to the hospital." This time the severity of the moment registered, and he scooped up Thomas and headed towards the car, gently trying to distract him by talking about a hole that Thomas had been digging in the front yard.

After situating Thomas and Kathleen in the car, Jack dashed back up the stairs and picked up Philip, their still sleeping three-year-old. Screams came from the back seat as Jack flew down Abercorn to DeRenne and turned onto Reynolds Street and into the Candler Emergency Room entrance. He slammed on brakes right outside the door and Kathleen jumped out, suddenly realizing she was still in her nightgown. Immediately, two men ran out with a wheelchair, grabbed both her arms, and sat her down. She looked at them confused until she remembered she was big and pregnant. They laughed when she told them it wasn't for her, but stopped once they heard the screams from the backseat.

A quick assessment from the doctors showed everything pointed to his appendix, and they prepped Thomas for surgery, did bloodwork, and wheeled him back. Jack went straight to his next worry: Kathleen. "I've got to get you something to drink. I don't want you going into labor just yet." Their eyes locked, and they shared all of their worries in that one look. It's amazing that when you love a person how much can be said to one another without even talking. Philip miraculously slept on Jack's shoulder, so they quietly said a prayer for Thomas' safety, the skill of the surgeons, and a speedy recovery. They began the Joyful Mysteries of the Rosary, since it was early Monday morning, and doing so gave them the comfort they needed.

The doctor found them after the surgery was complete and Thomas had been moved to recovery. He said Thomas had done great in surgery. His appendix was enlarged, but he was able to remove it without it rupturing. Thomas would need to stay at least two days in the hospital then he could go home. Also, Thomas' bloodwork indicated that he had type one hemochromatosis.

"Hemo what?" she asked, with a shaky voice.

"Hemochromatosis. It is a disorder in which your body stores too much iron."

"How did he get it?" Jack asked.

The doctor explained, "Well, it's a genetic disorder. Researchers think it started in Ireland during the potato famine. At that time, the Irish had a poor diet, so their bodies would conserve iron in order to survive. This caused a mutation in their genes. One in four people of Irish descent are carriers. But, his type only occurs if both parents are carriers, so both of you need to be tested and treated. I can order the blood test right now in the hospital and you can follow up with an endocrinologist. This is easy to treat through blood donations to decrease your iron level. At this point, Thomas does not need to worry about this, but it's good that he's aware of it for his future." She and Jack both made appointments with the doctor for the following week.

As the days flew by and Thomas returned home from the hospital, they settled down from all the excitement. She and Jack decided they would go on a "day date" to spend time alone together before the baby was due. Her mom came over and sat with the kids. They went to lunch downtown, caught a matinee movie, and had a 4 o'clock appointment with the endocrinologist. The meeting was to go over the preliminary blood work results and plan a course of action.

The doctor wasn't aware of the reasons behind them being tested and assumed they were worried about the baby they were expecting. He started explaining the disease, "Hemochromatosis is a big word for what we commonly call the Celtic Curse."

Kathleen immediately remembered the elderly nun in the cemetery at Kylemore Abbey who had proclaimed, "The Celtic Curse is a blessing, it means you are born with true Irish blood." She felt a tingle run up her spine, and had to concentrate to pay attention to the doctor.

"Well, only one of you have the disease, so this is good news for your baby," and he motioned towards her giant belly. Then he turned to Jack, "Looks like you're off the hook. Both parents have to be carriers for a child to have this disease. Kathleen, you will need to begin to follow-up yearly with me. And..." Kathleen didn't hear anything further. Everything was a blur. They stumbled out of the office and to the car and just sat there. Neither one of them said a word. Jack didn't start the car; they just sat.

Finally, he said, "I don't understand. Please explain this to me. Did I miss something? Please tell me this is all a huge mistake and I need to get retested. TALK TO ME!!!"

Her heart was beating out of her chest, "I don't know

what to say, Jack. My brain is trying to put the pieces together, too. I'm just as shocked as you."

"Am I Thomas' father?"

"Yes. Absolutely."

"Is there any chance, even a small one that I'm not?"

She was silent for what seemed like an eternity, then uttered just one word. "Ireland."

Jack held her stare, then his eyes drifted down to the Celtic Cross hanging from her neck. Shaking his head, he stormed out of the car leaving the door hanging open, and didn't glance back. He walked down DeRenne Avenue with its 5:00 bumper to bumper traffic. She watched as his figure became smaller and smaller and eventually disappeared. She waited another hour, just in case he came back. But as each minute passed, the worry that he may never return became a growing possibility.

The drive home was a blur. She walked into the kitchen and heard the laughter of her boys taking a bath. She yelled up to her mom that she was home and walked onto the back porch. Sitting in a rocker, she propped up her swollen feet. *What if Jack never comes back? I really can't blame him if he didn't. How did I let this happen? That one night. That one time. That one sin, has hurt so many people. Please, God, help me to make things right. Please bring Jack home to us.*

~

JACK CLIMBED into bed at 3 a.m. She pretended to be asleep but felt his every breath. She loved this man with all her heart and yet she was the one causing him so much pain. She could never take that away from him. He knew the truth, and only he could decide which road they would travel.

Her water broke at 5 a.m. God has a way of keeping everyone on their toes so they don't wallow in uncertainty for too long. Kathleen immediately started the "delivery plan," and to her surprise Jack was at her side, just like he had been for the last two deliveries.

Anne was born at 2:12 in the afternoon. She was an easy delivery since she was number three and came into the world with a graceful little smile. When all the nurses left, she and Jack locked eyes. "Congratulations, Daddy!" she said.

Jack just shook his head and tears welled in his eyes. "I was there, just like I am now, when Thomas came into the world. He is my child. I've raised him and I love him completely."

"He is your child. I'm so sorry, Jack." She said in between sobs. "Can you ever forgive me?"

"It's hard to be mad at you when I just watched you deliver our daughter, but you broke my heart yesterday. I just don't understand how you could have done this to me, to us."

"I didn't know, Jack. I didn't know that Thomas was…was…"

"Was what, not my child?"

"No, that Thomas was conceived before we were married. I was shocked. I made a mistake on my last night in Italy. I was coming home to tell you and to beg your forgiveness, but on the plane I realized that it was my sin to carry, not yours, and it would only bring you sadness. I didn't love him, and I would never, ever see him again."

"Well that was a hell of an error in thinking, wasn't it?"

"On the plane ride home, I realized that it would only hurt you if you knew. There's only you, Jack. You have all my love. Always have and always will."

"I never doubted your love for me, EVER! Hell, I still

don't. I was knocked back yesterday, but I saw that you were just as shocked. I don't want to know any more details. Really, I just want to get the thought of you in another man's arms out of my brain and pretend it didn't happen. Does anyone else know the truth?"

"Only one other person, and he is 3000 miles across the Atlantic Ocean. He has no idea about Thomas...and I intend to keep it that way," she said.

Jack nodded only once. "There is nothing more to discuss. I pray that over time, I'll forget all about it completely. I love you and all three of our children."

## GROWING CLOSER

True to his word, Jack never discussed Thomas' biological father. Kathleen never brought it up, either. As Thomas got older, Kathleen began to notice how much he looked like Quinn. Although they were almost identical, it wasn't just his appearance but also his mannerisms. Jack would never recognize the way Thomas' eyes lit up when he was excited about something, or the way he held a glass, or even the way he walked. Exactly like Quinn. She knew that Quinn would have been proud of Thomas, and it broke her heart to keep such a secret from him. But her first loyalty was to Jack, so she said nothing to Quinn.

She and Jack had two children after Anne: Lizzie then Christopher. Life was very hectic with five children under the age of ten. They remodeled the Jones Street house to accommodate their swelling numbers.

Each passing year brought Jack and Kathleen closer together. The accounting firm continued to depend on her, and as long she met her deadlines, they continued to send her work that she could do at home. Her boss joked that he had saved her desk for when her last child started school. This became a running joke at the firm because she and Jack tried to space their children two years apart so it appeared that she was always expecting.

When their youngest, Christopher, started kindergarten, Kathleen continued working from home. She enjoyed the much-needed time to organize their lives and their downtown home. Jack began walking home more and more for lunch, and they quickly discovered how nice it was to be alone in the house. For years, they went on weekend trips to be alone. They appreciated conversations without interruptions, a nice meal with wine, and the beauty of sleeping all night without a child crawling into their bed. But they found it much nicer to be alone together in their own home.

Through the passing years, Kathleen and Jack's family with small children became a family with many teenagers. She became more flexible and learned how to choose her battles. Her daily prayer life became a necessity and taught her how to control her worries about each child while remaining in control. Life changed as the children grew up, and the problems became more complex. But each battle was handled with love and respect. Through each change, Kathleen realized that she was changing, too.

Jack and Kathleen started to enjoy the benefits of living in downtown Savannah as a couple again. For years, all of their activities were family-oriented, but now they could leave the children at home with their oldest and go many places within walking distance. Long strolls through Savannah's historic squares were followed by romantic candlelight dinners. They listened to symphonies in the park with a picnic basket full of wine and hors d'oeuvres or went to art shows hosted by The Savannah College of Art and Design.

Often, Kathleen told Jack that they were blessed. She and Jack clung to each other, as well as their faith, while they raised their family. One by one, the kids left, but the two of them grew even closer. Romance sparkled amidst the chaos of raising a family, fueled by shared laughter. They hated to be apart.

# THE FINAL TEST

IRELAND

Present Day

No one knew about Brian's cancer. When the doctors told him the previous month that he was in the final stages and couldn't do anything more, Brian started preparing for the next few weeks. He wasn't afraid of dying, but he knew he had to make some plans. The first thing was to speak with a lawyer. He explained that he had a blood relative in the states who would be the legal heir to his estate, and changed his will, naming Kathleen Kenny Murray in Savannah, Georgia. She would take care of the land. The second thing he did was to invite the newly ordained Father Dillon to the farm. Brian explained his situation and made his confession. The kind priest gave him two sacraments that day: penance and last rites.

He was tying up his loose ends but now needed to get

word to Kathleen of his desire for her to take the Kenny property. He wrote her a short letter, enclosed a copy of the will, and asked Sara McMillon to mail it for him when she came to deliver her stew. God bless that woman. He gave a large sigh as he watched her walk down the sidewalk with his letter in hand. Now, everything was complete. He would focus on making himself comfortable for his last few days, weeks, or months. Little did he know that he would collapse outside that afternoon only to be found by the postal carrier? Now, Brian was sitting in the hospital waiting on a ride home.

When the E.R. doctors told Brian they had called Gray, he demanded his right to privacy. He informed them that he would NOT give permission for them to discuss his diagnosis with anyone. He wanted to spend his last few weeks peacefully and was upset that Gray had been notified. Why couldn't he just die in peace?

Gray had received the call from the E.R. doctor who explained that he needed to come and take his da home. Gray was about to explain that Brian wasn't his da, but he stopped himself. He had gotten in some trouble gambling in London and probably could use a little time away from the city. Hopefully, everyone would forget about his debts and misconduct. He walked into Brian's hospital room and heard the ole man talking crazy again about wanting to get home to the fairies. Good gosh! When would this man ever stop talking about the damn fairies? Brian's crazy talk was the reason he had left home 12 years ago.

When the doctors dismissed Brian, they gave Gray a bag full of Brian's medications which he proudly shoved right into the trash can. *He won't be needing any of this,* he thought as an evil grin spread across his face. As he was driving Brian home, he started thinking about how he could relax for the next few weeks without having to hang out with the old man. *Maybe if I can get him back in his room, I won't have to listen to his craziness,* he thought, but his plan had many gaps. As feeble as Brian was, his brain was sharp, and he shuffled to places around the property that he shouldn't be able to. Gray realized that he might be in over his head.

Time crept by slowly on the farm. If it weren't for being able to watch the telly, Gray would have gone insane. Brian had visitors that popped in at different times, so Gray had to be on his best behavior. Every week that goodie-goodie Mrs. McMillon would bring a huge pot of stew or soup that Brian would eat for the week. This week when she came, she gave Gray instructions to warm it up for Brian. "What do I look like, the maid?" he asked while taking the lid off to see what was inside. She popped the top of his hand with the wooden spoon and said, "You mind your manners, lad. Your da has been good to ye. You warm his food up once a day and bring it to him with hot tea. You mind me, lad."

*She's a scary one,* he thought. *I will have to watch my back with her prying eyes around*. He nodded and left the room.

Brian spent most of his days sitting in a rocking chair of sorts in his herb garden. The chair was made of sticks and vines and had been there for as long as he could remember. He had placed it under a makeshift shed that kept him dry during the many hours of rain. He talked to the world around him and wrote in a small notebook, scribbling down the ingredients to all of his herbal recipes.

He had written to Kathleen several times over the years, asking if she would consider coming back and taking care of the land. She always sent a sweet reply, telling him a few facts of her life in Savannah, saying she missed him, but she never agreed to return to Ireland. As he was getting older, he wished she had lived in Knock but firmly relied on the promise she had made him to take care of the Kenny land when he was gone.

He knew his days were numbered; the doctors had told him that the cancer was in its final stage. He had been told to come back when he could no longer manage the pain, but the beauty of his herbs was that they made the pain manageable. His days might be numbered, but he felt better than he had in years. He mixed together one of his mother's special tinctures, made a few additions, and took it three times a day. He didn't have to worry about the side effects of synthetic drugs, like nausea or even an overdose. Each day he was grateful for how his land took care of him.

Brian felt good and tried to keep busy. *It's no sense sitting around waiting to die,* he thought. His herb garden brought him joy. He spent his life following the examples of his mother and the herbs she had used in her remedies. Through the years, Brian nourished all of her plants and had improved many of them, making them more vigorous than ever. He added ingredients to make tinctures for different people in town. From hair growth to arthritis, his tinctures continued to help, and his herbs would remain hearty long after he was gone.

He pinched off a piece of his woad plant and grinned, thinking about his goats. They were drawn to woad, an immune system boosting plant that made them the healthiest goats in the county. However, he had to cage most of the plant to keep it away from the goats and available for the folks that needed it most. He laughed, thinking back of a run-in with the vet when his strong female goat was having problems kidding. The delivery had gone well at first but had abruptly stopped. The vet checked her and jumped back when he noticed her blue tongue. He started yelling "Plague!" while Brian explained that the goats had gotten into his woad plants. Although he used woad to build folks immunity, another everyday use was a natural blue dye. After examining two other goats, the vet settled down, and the kid was born shortly after. The story still made Brian chuckle.

His thoughts went to Gray and how he had been such a good lad when he was a boy. He shook his head because that lad was no longer. He had changed and became more and more agitated by the day. The two had a heated discussion the week prior about Gray's inheritance. He naturally assumed he would inherit everything since Brian didn't have any heirs. But Brian told him that there was an amendment to his signed will, and it had been filed away for safekeeping. He didn't tell him that Mrs. McMillon had mailed it to the States. "Kathleen will be getting the house and land, and you will get all the money in my savings account," Brian explained.

"You are giving that little chit all of this? She was only here a couple of weeks."

Brian was surprised that Gray was upset. "Why would you want this land? You haven't been home in years, and you hate it here?"

Gray narrowed his scorn-filled eyes, "This is not my home! But this land is worth a pretty penny." Then, shaking his head, he laughed mockingly. "You took a liking to Kathleen, didn't you? You been pining after her? You think she loved ya?"

Fury and disgust got the best of Brian, and he swung his cane in anger. He would have hit Gray square on the nose if he hadn't lost his balance. He fell hard onto the floor and landed, looking straight up at Gray, who said, "We'll see about all this, old man," and walked out of the room.

Brian lay still on the floor for a minute. He waited for his body to signal an injury. Nothing. He got up slowly. He had been around desperate men before, and Gray had all the signs. A man who had nothing to lose would have no recourse for his actions.

Brian came up with an idea. He may be old and dying, but he still had a fire in his belly. He was not going to sit back and let Gray get the last laugh. He thought of the woad plants and how they stained the tongue, then he pulled the tincture that he had been taking to ease his pain. He knew that if he added woad to his tincture, it could not hurt him in the least bit physically. The small amounts that he took would not even leave any blue stain on his tongue. However, large amounts would leave his tongue dark blue. He added it, said the Saint Michael prayer to himself, and asked Father Dillon back for a visit.

The young priest had come first thing the following morning. Brian wrote a letter, making sure the good priest witnessed him sign and date it, sealed it, had the priest sign the outside envelope, and gave it to him. He explained, "At my death, please give this letter to the coroner." Father Dillon agreed, thinking it was Brian's directions for his funeral.

That day, when Gray brought his stew, Brian pretended to be his most feeble self. He told Gray that he was not able to measure his medicine any longer and asked him to start giving him his tincture mixed in his tea. "Only five drops, my boy. Five drops keeps me heart pumping well, but any more might make it stop," but he knew that the tincture was harmless.

Gray's evil grin made Brian realize just how much the devil was on his heels. He sighed and thought, *I hope I'm wrong. I hope there is still some good left in that lad. But if there's not, I must make sure he doesn't stay in Knock. A man wanted for attempted murder will leave and never return. I just pray that I'm wrong.*

# WHISPERS IN THE NIGHT

It had been the longest few days of Kathleen's life. She took a long hot bath and replayed the week. *How in the world would this whole thing end with Quinn?* She toweled off, slathered her face with her nightly wrinkle cream, and put on her nightgown. As she walked into her bedroom, she glanced at Jack's side of the bed and let out a loud sigh, "Why aren't you home tonight?" she mumbled.

Knowing that she would fight sleep yet another night if she got into bed, she grabbed her book from the bedside table and went downstairs. She brewed a cup of chamomile tea, carried it to the living room, and snuggled on the couch with their dog, Beau. He burrowed in the blanket that covered her legs, and his warm little body comforted her a bit, so she dozed off.

Kathleen knew Brian had died before she ever got word. Strange as it was, just as he had explained when she was in Ireland, she had developed second sight after Thomas was born. Brian had come to her as she slept on the couch. He said her name, "Kathleen. Kathleen."

She answered, "Brian?"

"I'm dying, and I'm scared, Lass," he said.

"Oh, Brian. It's okay. You've lived a good and holy life, and you're so loved. God is waiting for you," she answered. "You can't hold; you must let go," and then there was silence. She rolled over, opened her eyes, and knew.

This wasn't the first time it had happened. At various times, different family members who had passed during the night had spoken to her. She figured out that she could communicate sometime in the state between being asleep and awake. If someone died during the day, she would get a feeling, but there was no interaction. She would always call or text the family to say hello, and then find out. "I can't believe you are calling right now," they would say. "Aunt Rachel passed during the night." She would nod into the phone, knowing their loved one's last thoughts but didn't dare share them with anyone.

Her senses were always working double time. Several of the downtown places that she loved now felt different. There were feelings in houses and buildings that she couldn't explain: some sad, some scared, and others happy. She started going to places that were new and staying in hotels that didn't have a past.

Her last trip to Rome had been a doozie. She had stayed up many nights trying to calm her feelings. Any average therapist would say she had issues that needed to be resolved, but she knew what they were. She also knew that prayer brought her peace.

Jack knew of her abilities, but she didn't share them with anyone else. He could always read her face and would ask her what was going on. It was nice to be able to talk about it to another person. Gradually, some of her children also started noticing strange things about her.

When Thomas was searching for a place to rent after graduation, he had asked her to go apartment hunting with him. They had gone to three not-so-wonderful apartments around Savannah. They were looking forward to seeing a cute little bungalow in the Ardsley Park area, but Kathleen was hit in the face with immense sadness as soon as they walked inside. She made it to the kitchen before telling Thomas and the realtor that she needed fresh air and had to wait outside. Thirty minutes later, when Thomas came out on cloud nine, she gently told him that he couldn't live there. She verified with the realtor, who confirmed that a very nasty murder had taken place in the house in the 1950s. Thomas had a million questions, but she just shrugged it off, saying the house had a weird vibe. To this day, Thomas asked her about her "vibe" when she walked into certain places. It was a gift that Kathleen had never asked for, but it had slowly become a part of her.

She closely watched Anne, wondering if she could also have this ability. When Kathleen felt something strange, she would look at Anne, darting her eyes around looking for the culprit. Kathleen would always ask her if she was alright, but Anne had never confided in her.

Kathleen knew she wouldn't be going back to sleep, so she got up for the day.

She turned down the hallway to the kitchen and stopped face to face with the Pink Lady. Kathleen was stunned and stood very still. The lady turned and moved away from Kathleen and down the hallway, so Kathleen could only see her back. Kathleen shouted, "Why don't you leave me the hell alone?" The lady stopped for the first time ever. Kathleen knew that she didn't want any interaction with a ghost, hovering motionless, and was relieved when she eventually disappeared out of sight. She hadn't realized she had been holding her breath until she exhaled and saw her hands trembling. Why was all of this happening now? Why had both Quinn and Brian contacted her from Ireland? She had to make sense of it all. She walked into the kitchen and glanced at the microwave clock that read 3 a.m., knowing it would be 8:00 a.m. in Ireland. Her heart hurt thinking about Brian, and she knew she must find a way to check on him. How could she do that without calling the police? Who could she call without sounding crazy? Then the obvious came to mind, Sara McMillon: Quinn's Mom. She grabbed her phone, pulled up Mrs. McMillon's contact, and was about to press the call button when she paused. What if she knew about Thomas? What if Quinn had talked to his mom? Jack asked Kathleen not to speak with anyone, and she had made a promise to him. What if Mrs. McMillon hated her? She put a coffee pod in their new Italian coffee machine and immediately smelled the aroma of courage. "I have to do this," she muttered and picked up her phone again and quickly pressed "call" before she changed her mind.

Kathleen rang the bakery and asked for Sara. When Mrs. McMillon came on the line, Kathleen was relieved that they talked like they had in the past, just like two old friends. Kathleen asked if Sara could do her a favor, then told her she had a bad dream about Brian. She asked if she could go and check on him, just to ease her mind. Mrs. McMillon told her this was the day for her to take him food, and she would let her know.

Kathleen walked to her closet and pulled out the shoebox from the top. Over the years, she had briefly read the letters in the box as they were delivered from Ireland. Although she had closed her heart to Ireland in order to live her life in Savannah, she had kept up with each person the best she could. She had always felt guilty when she wrote a brief reply to Brian, mainly telling him about her growing family. Still, she always sent her love and included her phone number if he needed her. She also kept in touch with Mrs. McMillon and even had calls from her a couple of times.

As she opened the lid, she saw Brian's Celtic Cross necklace. She had taken it off the day that she and Jack found out about Thomas' Hemocromatosis, knowing that Jack didn't need a constant reminder of her time in Ireland. She pulled the necklace over her head and started crying. "Sweet Brian," she said with sorrow. She arranged the letters from oldest to newest and started reading. The older letters were carefree, sharing about things in Knock; Quinn getting married, Mrs. McMillon opening up a bakery, and of course, he always mentioned the fairies. But the last four letters were almost urgent. She had remembered reading them and had put in a call to Mrs. McMillon, who said that he was just getting older and she would check on him. As she read them more intently, she noticed his desperation. He explained that the brownies had started helping him out, so he knew he would be dying soon. He also listed recipes for his tinctures and rubs and explained where he left things in the house for her. The last letter had arrived only the week before. The first page was a legal document. She quickly scanned it and realized it was a copy of Brian's will leaving his land to her. Along with it was an attorney's name in Ireland. She quickly flipped to the second page and noticed that it was a letter, the last one she would ever receive from Brian.

*Dear Kathleen,*

*I know that you are doing well. I feel it in me bones.*

*Gray has moved home. He said he wanted to take care of me in my old age but is doing anything but. He is angry all of the time. I told him of the revisions to my will to leave the property to you, and he is searching through all of my drawers, looking for it. I'm vera happy that I had Mrs. McMillon mail it to you two weeks ago.*

*I hope that you realize our small amount of time together gave me more joy than you will ever know. I think about you as the daughter I never had.*

*Remember your promise to me. It's now time to fulfill it.*

*Love, Brian*

She barely heard the phone ringing over her sobs, but she ran to pick it up. Mrs. McMillon said that she had been to Brian's house. When she delivered the soup, she found him dead in his garden, sitting in his chair.

When Father Dillon found out about Brian's death, he took the letter to the coroner's office as promised. The coroner looked at the letter that Brian had dated ten days prior, opened it carefully, and began reading. His hands started shaking violently, and he walked straight to the phone and called the Garda.

Father Dillon picked up the letter and started reading.

"To Whom This May Concern,

If you are reading this, I am dead. Please have the coroner take a look at my tongue. If it's blue, call the Garda."

He stopped and looked at the coroner, who nodded and said, "His tongue was so blue, it looked black."

The following paragraphs of Brian's letter explained his cancer, how he had died of natural causes, his doubts about Gray, his goats, and the vet story, and his final test on Gray in which the coroner now knew that Gray had failed. Then it told the Garda to pick Gray up for intent to kill. It was signed and dated and ended with a smiley face.

# NOT ON THE HOME TURF

Jack looked at the paper with his conference schedule on it, crushed it into a ball, and tossed it in the trash. He and Kathleen had always feared this day would come but had never prepared for it. He knew that he was making a decision on a whim, but the flights from London to Ireland took little over an hour, and he needed some answers.

The plane landed in Knock, and Jack hailed a taxi to McMillon Farms. As the car drove through the farm gates, Jack suddenly wondered what he was doing there. *I'm not on the home playing field. This is literally another man's home,* he thought, but as he traveled farther down the drive, he realized that he was not on the little Irish farm that he was expecting.

"A corporate office. Really?" he muttered out loud.

The taxi driver overheard and answered, "McMillon has become quite the corporation in town, don't ya know? They are actually McMillon Farms and Bakery and employ half the town, yes they do." He drove to the front of a large building and let Jack out.

Jack walked into an impressive office and found out that Quinn McMillon had left for the day. He put on his best "good ole boy smile" and started sweet-talking the young and perky receptionist. He explained that he was from the States and had really hoped to meet Mr. McMillon. He flashed that smile again and added a little wink for good measure.

Finally, she conceded, but not because of his good looks. "You remind me so much of my da, I'll let ya know where he was off to today. He went to Dowling's."

*I remind her of her Da? Ouch! I've really got to get back to the gym. If only my knees didn't hurt all the time, and my back, and everything else. Hell, her da is probably in better shape than I am. Dang it!* He thought to himself.

Dowling's was a crowded, yet seemingly friendly, establishment. He found a stool at the end of the bar facing the room full of people. Jack didn't have to ask around for Quinn; he spotted him right away. *Well, I'll be,* he thought. *Thomas looks just like him.* He was looking in the face of his son, only twenty-eight years older. Jack decided to wait and watch while drinking a pint, but his one pint soon turned into three. An hour and a half later, Quinn got up and walked towards the door.

Jack threw his money on the bar and started after Quinn. When Jack came running out the door, Quinn was waiting on the other side. He grabbed Jack by the collar. "What's the matter with you, man? You've been watching me all bloody night. You need to back off."

All of the emotions that Jack had held in for the last few days boiled to the surface. He knocked Quinn's hands from his shirt and pinned him against the outside wall. "Hardly the advice I'd expect from someone like you."

Quinn looked confused but was very aware of Jack's strength holding firm. "I think you've got the wrong guy, mate."

Jack slowly let go. "I definitely don't have the wrong guy. I knew who you were the second I walked into the bar. You look just like my son."

Recognition played across Quinn's face. He had seen this man before. He was the dad from Kathleen's family picture. Quinn nodded and tentatively offered his hand. "Quinn McMillon."

Jack looked at his extended hand for a moment, then grasped it. "Jack Murray." The two men summed each other up.

"It's vera nice to meet you, Jack," Quinn said with a reassuring smile. "How bout a cup of the good stuff back at my house?"

Jack slightly tilted his head while he pondered the situation. Narrowing his eyes, he slowly nodded and followed Quinn to his truck. When they got to the farm, they went in through the kitchen door and straight to the table. Quinn took out two small Mason jars, filled them with milk, then brought out a plate of his mom's scones. They both took a huge bite, a big gulp of milk, and sighed with pleasure.

"Tell me, what can I help you with?" Quinn asked.

"Kathleen has no idea I'm here. In fact, no one does. I just had to know."

"Know what?" Quinn asked.

"Know that you're a good person before I let my son become a part of your life." Jack's voice cracked with emotion. Where did that come from? Thomas was a grown man. Why was he feeling so protective? Do you ever stop being protective of your children?

Jack continued, "I came to the farm looking for you today and was told that you were at the bar. I figured you to be a drunk who went to the bar every night, but I just sat and watched. You sipped on the same pint all night. You gave money from your pocket to the couple with a baby. She had the baby in a bar, by the way. Very weird in the States. She hugged you repeatedly. Then you crossed the room to help the older female server get a tray of heavy glasses down. Then you sat with your hand on the shoulder of an older gentleman who cried quietly." Quinn simply nodded. "You impressed me, and I don't impress easily. I really don't know if I should hug you or punch you in the face for loving Kathleen."

"I'm not in love with your wife. I lost the love of my life, and I can imagine what you must be going through. I'd have crossed a million oceans to keep my Maura beside me." Jack nodded because that's exactly how he felt. Quinn continued. "I just don't understand how she could have kept this from me."

Jack answered, "Kathleen loves her family with all her heart and protects them at all costs. She was protecting me. If you blame anyone, you should blame me because I loved Thomas too much to share him."

They sat in silence for a long time, contemplating the situation. Quinn finally added voice to his thoughts, "Like you, I have had the love of a wife that I would lay down my life for; God bless her sweet soul. I also have been blessed with children, so I understand, but it doesn't make the blow any less." They both stood and shook hands, ready to call it a night. "I am happy to have met ya. Why don't ya hunker down here for the night, and I'll get you a ride to town in the mornin?"

The following day, after Jack had left, Quinn felt unsettled. He asked his son, Dillon, to stop by the house to help him process his emotions. As Dillon entered the kitchen and took one look at his father, he knew that he must take him on a ride to get him to open up. They drove the golf cart down the road to a shady spot by the lake and sat quietly watching the dragonflies skim the surface.

Dillon started the conversation, "I haven't seen you like this in a vera long time. Are you alright?"

When Quinn started talking, his emotions came out all at once. He felt his eyes misting and was surprised by the tears. He told Dillon everything, beginning from when his father had died all the way to his visit with Jack. He was so upset with the situation and the anger that it was bringing to his heart. Dillon listened intently until Quinn shrugged, looking sad and depleted.

"Do you agree that sin has consequences that affect everyone, even if you can't see them?" Dillon asked. Quinn shook his head yes. Dillon smiled, "Well, so does love. I'm not sure if you remembered the homily last week, but it was about choices."

Quinn replied, "Well, as a matter of fact, I do. It was that homily that put me in this predicament."

"Hear me out. Right now, you have a choice. You can either hold onto bitterness, be angry with Kathleen, and forgo a relationship with Thomas. Or you can see God's hand in this and choose love. You have another son. Although you may have wanted to know him much earlier, it was God's timing, not yours. Embrace it now and get to know him."

Quinn smiled and looked at his son. "When did you get to be so smart?" he asked as he felt the weight of the world being lifted from his shoulders. He ruffled his hair like he did when he was a boy, and they drove back to the farm.

# THE WAY TO A MAN'S HEART

"You did what???" Kathleen shouted.

Jack had walked in the door only ten minutes earlier and couldn't wait to tell Kathleen about his quick trip to Ireland. "Although the Irish are a strange lot, I liked him."

"But why? Why didn't you tell me you were going?" she asked.

Jack answered, "I had to make sure that he was a good person before we told Thomas. I know Thomas. He will go looking for him, Kate."

Jack was the only person in the world who called her Kate. He used this nickname when she was worried or upset about something, and it totally disarmed her. It meant, "I've got you. Everything is okay."

"Well, how did it go?" Kathleen asked. "Tell me everything."

Jack talked about his visit. He was impressed with McMillon Farms. He told her about how he had met Quinn and actually had stayed the night at his farm. She couldn't put her finger on her feelings. Was it worry? As a mother, she usually had control of most situations, but she had no control of what was to come.

"Will Thomas be okay, Jack? Will he hate me?" Kathleen asked.

"Thomas will NEVER hate you. It will be quite a blow for him, but he's a strong man, and he needs to know. This is his life and his future. We just love him through it and stand by any decision he makes." But even as Jack was saying this, he had his doubts.

Thomas was such a sweet child growing up. He was their only child with dark hair and always had a smile on his face. He was a bit quiet but was always the big brother protecting his four younger siblings. The girls always needed Thomas' help more than the boys because they were cursed with the Murray family's quick wit and sharp tongue. At every UGA football party, the girls would inevitably make someone angry, and Thomas, always the diplomat, had to come to their rescue. It became the family joke that he should have opened a meditation studio to calm hostile situations.

When Thomas was little, he loved digging in the dirt, learning about plants, and finding what each needed to survive. The nurseries were his playgrounds, and as he grew into a young man, the Murray's yard was transformed into a well-maintained and beautiful garden. At least once a year, their garden was voted "yard of the month" by the Historic Savannah Garden Club. They were always asked to be on the Hidden Gardens North of Gaston Street tour in Savannah, too. Thomas even talked her into planting a small herb and vegetable garden that produced enough veggies to keep her out of the grocery store. He was nicknamed the "plant whisperer."

After high school graduation, it was no surprise that he took off to Abraham Baldwin Agricultural College, located in Tifton, a small city in southern Georgia. He completed his education in Agricultural Technology and System Management, which combined science and agriculture for effective crop production.

Thomas met Clare at noon Mass at the cathedral. She had just graduated with a teaching degree from Saint Mary's at Notre Dame. She was snagged up quickly by the Diocese of Savannah to teach in one of its parochial schools. She was bright, happy, and very much in love with Thomas. They were married last June and lived on the outskirts of Savannah.

On Christmas, while opening presents, Kathleen and Jack found a small box labeled "Mom and Dad." They sat by each other while they opened it. Inside was an ultrasound picture of their first grandchild. They looked at Thomas and Clare, who were beaming proudly. The due date was September 1.

The week after Jack's return from Ireland, Kathleen invited Thomas and Clare to dinner. Lizzie and Christopher both had plans, so she set the table outside in the garden. The spring afternoon was chilly but comfortable, the garden was in bloom, and Jack lit the outside fireplace. If there was a perfect setting to tell one's child he was conceived out of wedlock by a stranger in Ireland then this was it. Her stomach rolled with nerves.

True to his word, Jack had never asked for details and would be hearing things for the first time. How would this day end? Would everybody hate her for her past sins and the secrets that were kept?

They arrived at 5:00 and had drinks and appetizers while waiting for dinner. Thomas' favorite meal was chicken parmesan, so it was a no-brainer that she would make that dish. The way to a man's heart is through his belly. . . maybe the meal would soften his heart.

"Do I smell chicken parm? What's the occasion?" Thomas asked.

"I just love you, that's all," she answered.

They had a lovely meal, then moved by the fire for dessert and Irish coffee. Once she thought about it, she probably should have just served coffee minus the Irish part. It might turn the mood sour, but it was too late to worry about that. She was shocked when Jack started the conversation. "Thomas, there is something your mom and I need to tell you."

Thomas and Clare looked at each other and appeared genuinely scared. Jack continued, "God blessed your mother and me when He gave you to us. You changed us from a couple to a family and have continued to bless us for 28 years. In every sense of the word, I am your father, but biologically I am not. That person lives in Ireland." Clare stood up and came and sat by Thomas and grabbed his hand. He looked at her and patted it, then turned his attention back to Jack, who continued speaking. "I've only met him recently, and he seems like a nice guy. He didn't know you existed until last week and probably has as many questions as you. I realize this is a shock, but we love you so much and want you to know the truth."

Her heart had never loved Jack the way it did at that moment. He protectively took the brunt of everything for her. Thomas looked from Jack to Kathleen and burst out laughing. It scared her, and she thought that he might think they were joking. Finally, Thomas said, "I'm fine. Just give me a minute, please," and he walked towards the back of the garden. She didn't realize she was crying until Clare handed her a towel. She smiled and took her hand.

Thomas walked back to their group, sat down, and took Kathleen's other hand. "For as long as I can remember, I would ask you both why I was so different from the rest of the family. You always told me I was special. All of my siblings look alike, with sandy hair and tanned skin. Whenever one of them was spotted around town, I would hear people say, 'There goes a Murray kid.' No one ever said that about me. My dark hair and fair skin were different. But that wasn't the least of it. All of you, and please don't take this the wrong way, are feisty. Y'all are quick-tempered and have big personalities. Our family was always the loudest ones rooting for one of our siblings at a sporting event, or at the St. Patrick's Day Parade, or even just trying to be quiet in church. I would be the one to diffuse an argument or quiet the bunch. Our family is so wonderful and works as one big unit, using each other's strengths and helping with each other's weaknesses, so I always had my part. Kudos to both of you for making each one of us feel so loved and respected." He paused, collecting his thoughts, and continued, "Mom, remember how I always joked with you saying, 'Are you sure I wasn't adopted?' when I was the only one doing something different? Like when we led the Christmas carols and all of you were fighting for the front, and I was fighting for the back? Or the many, many other things. I would always look to you and mouth those words. We would giggle because you saw it too. But now it makes so much sense. I am not even shocked. It's like I'm finally validated."

"My sweet boy," she ran her hand along the side of his face. "I'm so sorry."

He nodded slowly, then said, "I'm fine, really I am, and I

love you both. I'm just...Well, I guess I'm just curious." He stopped to ponder his next words. "I want to go to Ireland."

She felt a tugging at her heart and knew that it was time to tell the whole story of her time in Ireland, the story that she hadn't told a soul. She turned to Jack and asked him if that would be okay, and he nodded, so she began. For the next hour, she talked of Ireland and her time there, from beginning to end. Talking about it gave it life, and she found herself longing to be there again. She wanted to share all that she loved about Ireland with Thomas, and she prayed that someday she could share it in person with Jack. Her secret had finally been shared, and a burden had been lifted. Thomas knew the truth, and however he decided to proceed was entirely up to him.

# LOVE OF FAMILY AND FRIENDS

The dream came again that night, and she found herself back in Ireland. "Where is it? I can't find it anywhere!" Kathleen was frantically searching as she moved past the long stone fence. But there was something very different, what was it? As she came upon the garden, a young man was digging in the soil, but he was blurry. She ran as fast as she could, trying to reach him, but couldn't close the distance. She was frantic and gasping for breath as something began to shake her. "Kathleen. Kathleen. You're having it again. Wake up." She opened one eye to the darkness of her bedroom and tried to get her bearings. Jack quietly asked her if she was alright before turning over and falling back to sleep.

She looked at the bedside clock that read 5:30 and knew that she was up for the day. The dreams had returned, and sleep deprivation was starting to affect her again. She remembered this feeling 28 years ago, and she also remembered what she must do to end the dream, but she wasn't ready to go back to Ireland. Not yet.

She went to the kitchen and put on a pot of coffee, wondering who the young man digging in the soil might be. Was it a younger Brian? She couldn't make sense of it. As she waited for the sun to make its graceful entrance, she said her morning prayers and looked through the daily readings. She heard the birds before seeing them, so she took her coffee out to the back porch. She rarely took the time to sit in the swing anymore. Oddly, the things she once did every day became things far from her daily routine. She was surprised to see that the cardinals had returned and that there were little baby birds everywhere. She reached way back in her memory to the songs she would sing to her children as they were swinging, and she began to sing out loud. Sure enough, the birds became still and seemed to pay attention. Somehow, they eased her mind from the disturbing dream.

Kathleen remembered Mrs. Murray saying that cardinals came when young children were in the home. She wondered if other reasons could have brought the birds back. She started researching cardinals by looking through several books. One book that stood out to her the most said a cardinal represents a loved one who has passed, and they usually show up when they are missed the most. They also seem to know when someone is going through a difficult time and come to reassure them that they will always be in that person's life.

The next day, when Kathleen took her coffee out to the swing, she started talking. People had thought her to be a bit crazy for years, so it wouldn't surprise anyone to see her talking to the birds. Many great saints, over time, had spoken to animals, and they weren't all weird. Although she was far from saint material, the thought justified her actions.

"Hey Brian," Kathleen said. "You got my attention. I really

don't understand these dreams, but I know that all will be well in my heart. I know that everything happening with Thomas will end exactly as it should because everyone involved has his best interests at heart. I haven't forgotten about you, and I know you are fine, too. You don't have to keep checking on me, although I do enjoy the visit. And, I'm really, really happy you didn't come to visit in the form of a magpie." She looked around at the birds, laughed softly, and walked further into the garden.

She made her way to the vegetables they had planted the week before to make sure the downtown squirrels, who were kept fat and happy with the food from the tourists, were keeping away from her seedlings. Her thoughts drifted back to the family dinner the previous night and how Jack had told the kids everything about Thomas. They were upset that they didn't get to see Thomas before he left for Ireland, and each had questions.

"How is Thomas? Is he okay?"

"Did he really just hop on a plane the next morning?

"What does this mean, exactly?"

"Why didn't you tell anyone?"

All were excellent questions that they answered one by one, until Anne stood up from the table, looked right at Jack, and said, "How are you so okay with this? Your wife slept with another man, and you sit there all calm. Am I missing something?" Then she glared at Kathleen and left the room.

"Awkward!" Philip said. They all smiled at him and started clearing the table. Each child, except Anne, hugged Kathleen and Jack goodbye and left the dining room. Anne had walked out to the garden and was sitting on a bench gazing at the fountain. Kathleen looked at Jack, shook her head, and walked outside. Anne grunted when she saw her mother coming.

Kathleen started the conversation, "I'm sorry, Anne. I'm sorry that you're upset. Parents aren't perfect."

"Are you kidding me, Mom? Parents aren't perfect? That's how you explain screwing around? I love Thomas, and I love Daddy. They have to be crushed. And you're gonna say, 'Parents aren't perfect.' Give me a break!"

"I made a mistake," Kathleen said. "But I'm not going to say that I regret it. I wouldn't have Thomas had I not. I'm not asking for your forgiveness, but I have asked for forgiveness from those whom I've needed to…God in confession and your dad."

Anne said, "Do you remember when I asked you if I could study abroad this past year? You told me it was too dangerous for a young woman to be abroad right now. And yet you went to Ireland by yourself? What's that phrase? 'Do as I say; not as I do.'"

"It was different then, and my parents didn't have to worry about human trafficking," Kathleen argued. "You have had the luxury of traveling, both with our family and on your high school graduation trip. I don't owe you any explanations for my actions. Once you have your own children, you might understand this better. You don't have to agree with me, or even like me right now, but you are not going to be disrespectful to me."

"Whatever, Mom, I'm outta here!"

Kathleen walked around the garden and settled on a bench by the herbs. She leaned over and rubbed her hand down the stalk of both the rosemary and basil plants. They instantly gave off the earthly aroma that she loved as she closed her eyes and sighed. Why was being a parent so hard?

Why did she need to explain her past to her children? It was none of their business. She had been a wonderful mother to all five of them. Shame on Anne for the guilt trip and turning the tables to make it all about her and studying abroad.

She started thinking about a saying that she used quite often as the children got older. "You're only as happy as your saddest child." She knew that she would need to talk this through with Anne. She had to acknowledge the fact that her past actions had repercussions. And, right now, Anne's anger was a big one.

Another repercussion Kathleen worried about was the tribe's reaction. Her longtime friends had made a pact not to withhold secrets from one another, so how would they handle hers? She was dreading her Wednesday lunch and was sad that this was the first time she felt that way. No one likes to admit their imperfections, and the tribe was going to hear many of hers.

It just so happened to be her turn to choose the lunch spot. She knew it would need to be somewhere that she was comfortable, so she decided on the Pink House. The downstairs bar had the feeling of walking onto an old sailing ship. A dark planked bar, made from reclaimed wood, still held the smell of seaweed and brought to mind adventures. The old brick walls dated to the late 1700s when the house was built. The finishing touch was subdued lighting that made patrons feel cozy and relaxed.

After they all had their first drinks in hand, Kathleen began: "I have something to tell y'all." All eyes were on her, scared eyes waiting for details. "Do you remember my trip to Ireland?" There were nods all around the table. "I told you that I met a really cool friend, Q, that lived in Knock, and we spent a good bit of time together?" They nodded. "Well, that friend was a male." Their expressions changed as they recalled the stories and experiences Kathleen had told them. But just like sins of omission, she had left out a few details about her time in Ireland. She continued, "On our last night in Rome, we slept together. It meant nothing to either of us, emotionally. I know that sounds cliché, but it's true. At any rate, when Thomas was five and had his appendicitis attack, we found out that Jack was not his biological father." There were gasps, some tears, and Jan started laughing hysterically. She always did that when she was nervous. It was hell to sit by her at a funeral.

"Q stands for Quinn. We told Thomas the truth, and he is in Ireland right now, meeting Quinn. I would die if you heard this from anyone else, and I trust you to please keep it to yourself." One by one, they stood up and hugged her, which turned into a giant group hug. Kathleen instantly felt the unconditional love of each of her friends.

"Well, I need another drink. You girls are gonna kill me," said Maggie as she ordered martinis for the table. No one had the nerve to tell her they all hated martinis, but Kathleen felt this might be the first time she could use one.

## DOUBLE TAKE

After flying through the night from Savannah to Knock, Thomas was ready for a good meal and a long nap. He checked on both the Uber and Lyft apps when he landed, but the closest driver was in Dublin. He walked out front and found a waiting cab.

"Name's Harry," said the elderly driver. "Where ye from and where ye going?"

"To Knock."

"Where about in Knock?"

"Somewhere to get a good breakfast."

"Where ye from, Yank?"

"A city in the States called Savannah, in Georgia."

"I once met a young lady from Savannah, Georgia. Pretty young lassie." Then he eyeballed Thomas in his rearview mirror. "Harrumph"

*Did he really just harrumph? Is that something that all Irish do?* Thomas wondered. He was dropped at a hole-in-the-wall restaurant that smelled wonderful. Walking inside, he noticed a large, ugly dog that everyone seemed to love. They called him Bear. As Thomas settled into the only open booth, he began to feel the stares. At first, he questioned himself, thinking that he was just an unfamiliar face, but when the lady at the booth beside him stood up and openly gave him a once over, he knew. *All of these people know my secret,* he thought with embarrassment.

He kept his head down the rest of the time, and after eating a hearty breakfast, he hit the streets. The one and only Bed and Breakfast had a sign in the window, "Be back by 4 o'clock", so he decided to follow the steeple to the Shrine of Our Lady of Knock.

Every August, his mom told the story of her great-grandfather and Knock, Ireland. She made a delicious meal, usually Irish stew, and entertained their family with many tales about the Irish people. After dinner, they would go outside, to the old rosary garden, and say the rosary. Clare thought it was hysterical last year, watching him and Philip pushing each other on the stones that seemed so far apart when he was a boy.

Thomas' steps quickened as he approached the shrine, but as soon as he came upon the entrance, he began to stroll, lost in his thoughts. He had missed morning Mass and began to wander the property. He noticed confessions were being held and walked into one of the many confession rooms. A young priest welcomed him but gave him a confused look. He started to say something, but Thomas began, "Bless me, Father, for I have sinned. It's been three weeks since my last confession. My sins are, well, my sin is doubt. I know doubt comes from not trusting God completely, but you see, I just found out last week that my biological father lives in Ireland. On a whim, I jumped on a plane to come find him. I trust in

God's plan but can't imagine that God's plan would bring me so far from home."

The priest sat for a second, rubbed his hand under his chin, then said, "You coming home reminds me of the story of Joseph and Israel in Genesis 46. You are the lost son that has come back to his father. Continue to follow the path God lays out for you and trust Him."

Thomas walked into Dowling's bar, looked around slowly, and headed to a barstool. At 3 o'clock midday, every seat was full, and every eye was on him.

The bartender greeted him, "Hiya, the name's Sean. What can I do you for?"

"I'll have a pint," Thomas said.

Everyone continued to stare, and a couple of people even got out of their seats to look at him. After all of the rubber-neckers that morning at breakfast, he was tired of being under the scrutiny of the people of Knock. "Does every stranger in town get the effin close and personal stares?" Thomas asked.

"Nah, mate, it's just uncanny, especially for the older ones that grew up with Quinn. You've been the talk of the town since you went to breakfast tis mornin. Take a look over there at the photo," he said, pointing to a picture on the wall.

Thomas walked closer to the photograph and saw that it read "Hurling Champs Knock 1995". A happy group of young men were on the field, and right in the center stood a man identical to Thomas. He stumbled back to his seat, looked at Sean, and said, "Good gosh. I look just like him."

"That you do, mate. That you do. Just like he spit you out," Sean said.

Thomas shook his head and sighed, "I've never looked like anyone in my family before."

"Irish genes are strong, but the ale is stronger. Looking like you might need that today, eh? Enjoy your draught, and I'll be back in a bit," Sean told him.

After a little while, the bar went quiet. Thomas turned to see the older version of himself walking into the room. He smiled as they made eye contact, and Quinn walked straight to him. He was confident and sturdy, and Thomas could tell by his eyes that he was a kind man. He wore overalls and a kerchief around his neck and probably had come straight from work. When Thomas stood, he gave him a once over and stuck out his hand.

"Quinn. Quinn McMillon."

"Thomas. Thomas from America."

"Sean called and told me that you were here. Come with me, Thomas from America; I think we have a lot to discuss." They walked out front and climbed in an old truck. Thomas only had a hiking backpack, so he threw it in the back.

"I guess this is quite a shock," Quinn said.

"You have no idea. I just found out about you last week and had to see for myself," Thomas answered. "I had no idea how much I looked like you, but the whole town sure noticed the resemblance."

Quinn replied, "I didn't know until recently, either. I was actually making plans to come to you. Your mum called and said she told you about me and asked me to hold off on coming to America. She had a feeling you were heading this way. Are you well?"

Thomas started to answer, "Oh, yes sir. The flight was great and…"

"No, are you well? Do you have a happy life?" Quinn asked.

"Oh! Yes, I have a very happy life." Thomas said. "I am

married. Her name is Clare, and she is a teacher. I definitely don't deserve her, but she overlooked that. We are expecting our first child in September. I have a wonderful family, and I love what I do. So, yes, I am happy."

Quinn looked over at Thomas with a tear in his eye. "You're gonna be a da. I'm so happy the Lord has blessed you so."

Thomas smiled, "That's what my mom always says."

"How is your mom?" Quinn asked.

"Well, right now, she is crazy worried about me. She thought that the news of you would be such a shock to me and that I would hate her. But it's odd. I'm not upset at all. I just have a lot of questions."

They drove further and further into the countryside and pulled into a large entrance gate that read "McMillon Farms." There were crops on each side of the road.

"You grow barley?" Thomas asked.

Quinn pulled the truck to a stop and turned to look at him. "What do you know of barley?"

Thomas laughed, "Agriculture is my first love. I graduated with that as my degree from college, and I work with farmers in the States. Every summer, for as long as I can remember, I worked the barley harvest with a family in Idaho. My mom had an old school friend who married a farmer from Idaho. Once she saw how passionate I was about farming, she arranged for me to spend my summers with them. And once they saw what I could do, they asked me back each year. I didn't know that you were a farmer." Then he laughed harder. "That explains so much."

"Well, I'll be," Quinn said, shaking his head. "My blood truly runs through your veins."

McMillon Farms ran for acres and acres. Further than the

eye could see, the golden barley swayed in every direction. They rode through the fields that opened to a large farmhouse, parked, and went into the house's side door that led straight to the kitchen. The house was quiet but had a warm, lived-in feeling. It reminded Thomas of his home growing up. The only word to describe it was "family."

Thomas asked, "Are you married? Have children? I asked my mom, but she didn't know."

"I am a widower, just shy of a year. We have three children: two girls and a boy. The girls are both local and work with the farm, but my boy does not," Quinn said.

Thomas asked further, "Does he not enjoy farming?"

Quinn thought before answering, then said, "When I met your mother, I was lost. Not physically but spiritually. My da had just passed, and he had given up on his faith. It seemed to trickle down to his children. Anyway, your mother is a headstrong woman."

"Don't I know it," Thomas replied.

"She wouldn't let me off the hook. She made me step up to my Catholic faith, go back to church, receive the sacraments, and make things right with the Lord. She reset my compass, so to speak. With that, I was able to find my bride, the love of my life, and raise my children as strong Christians. I guess I did such a fine job that our son was called to the priesthood. There hasn't been a new local priest in County Mayo for a very long time, but he is right here at Our Lady of Knock, and I'm so proud," Quinn said.

Thomas smiled, thinking about the priest's face when he had walked into confession. "I hope to meet him and your daughters."

"Oh, you will. Your brother and sisters," Quinn said.

Thomas took that in for a few seconds. It almost felt

disloyal to his family to call someone else his brother and sisters. His feelings were exposed, and he felt pretty sure that Quinn could read his emotions. But they just began to talk easily. Quinn told him about his family. His mom opened a bakery on the back of the property. She supplied bread to many grocery stores around Ireland and shipped cakes, pies, and pastries worldwide. Thomas smiled, vaguely remembering the McMillon Bakery boxes that came in the mail each Christmas.

Quinn's brother had married and moved to the outskirts of Dublin. He farmed his land, and together they ran McMillon Farms through separate locations. They both grew barley but had run into some problems recently. Quinn mentioned that he would love to get Thomas' opinion once he settled in.

The first night was quiet. Quinn said he had to be on the tractor each morning by 4 a.m., so he went to bed at 6 p.m. Thomas was jet-lagged, which worked perfectly for him. When he woke the following morning, Quinn had left him a note on the kitchen table.

*Grab some coffee and show yourself around the farm.*
*Big party tonight to meet your kin. Da*

Thomas wasn't sure how he felt about Quinn signing as Da, but it was nice just the same. Sitting beside the note was a set of keys. He walked outside of the kitchen and saw a golf cart of sorts with a flatbed attached. He drove around for almost two hours, stopping to take in the scenery. The crops were golden and lush and smelled of fresh earth and rain. As he continued down the road, the first thing he came to was a large building that looked to be offices. On one side of it sat a row of small cottages with little manicured lawns and blooming plants. Just past that sat a large building with a loading dock full of delivery trucks and a sign outside that read McMillon Bakery. He decided to stick his head in to take a look.

As he opened the door, he was met with the sweet aroma of fresh bread and cakes. He smiled and walked in further. A lady approached him with a huge grin, put her hand in the crook of his arm, and said, "Come with me, please." He was about to explain who he was but decided to just follow. She walked him down a long hallway with glass windows overlooking the bakery floor, turned at the end into a hall with several offices, and entered the first one.

An older lady stood up, put her hand to her mouth, and tried to contain her emotions but was unsuccessful. She reached both her hands out to him, and with tears running down her face said, "Come and meet your gram, boy." He liked her immediately and went straight into her arms. They sat and talked for more than an hour, and when he left, he took a bag of goodies, just like he did when his grandparents treated him to Krispy Kreme doughnuts. The thought made him smile. No matter how old you are, there is nothing better than a grandparent's love.

As Thomas drove away, he saw a lake with small fishing boats pulled to the edge. A couple of boys were fishing on the bank, and they were anxious to show him their catch. They told him that when they didn't have school, they were allowed to work with their da and fish while he was on the tractor. Their ma would cook the fish up at night in a cast iron pan, and they loved it. Thomas asked about their school, and they described a happy place. Math and science were their hardest subjects because their teacher was frequently sick. The school was trying to find a replacement, but there weren't many teachers in the area. Meanwhile, parents were taking turns teaching the class. He thought of Clare because she would love teaching these bright young boys.

Thomas moved along the side of the extended property, towards the front of the massive piece of land, and thought how nice it would be to see an aerial view of the property. At one point, he stopped in the middle of the path and was surrounded by barley. He closed his eyes, and the smell of fresh earth, growth, and life filled his senses. It was the happy feeling that he always had when he was outdoors: the feeling of being one with nature.

## WELCOME TO THE FAMILY

Quinn threw Thomas a welcome home party. He met most of the townspeople, but more importantly, his Irish siblings. Quinn's daughters, Colleen and Regan, were bright and sweet and instantly went into "mother mode," trying to take care of him, which made him feel welcomed. The kitchen door swung open, and Thomas noticed the priest from confession the day before. "Oh, there's Dillon, our brother," Regan said and introduced the two men. They both smiled at each other.

"We've actually already met," Thomas said.

Dillon nodded, extended his hand and said, "It's vera nice to see you again. How are you holdin up?"

"Couldn't be better. Your family is amazing," Thomas said which made both Regan and Colleen beam.

Dillon lifted his pint and said, "Let's celebrate. To our family!" Cheers went up, and glasses were emptied.

No one noticed Leah had wandered into the festivities, through all of the gaiety, until she was standing in front of

Thomas. "So it's true. I had to see him with me own eyes. He looks just like his da."

Thomas turned to his siblings in confusion as Quinn seemed to appear out of thin air. "Leah, I'd like you to meet my son, Thomas."

Leah turned her nose up at Thomas and her attention straight to Quinn. "So, that's how it's gonna be? This....boy tarnished me sister's good name. You are choosing him over Maura?"

Quinn answered, "I'm blessed to have another son. I would never deny him. You must know, in your heart, that Maura wouldn't have wanted me to."

She narrowed her eyes at Quinn, then to Thomas, turned, and walked out of the party. The crowd was quiet until Quinn motioned to the musicians, and the music started playing. Thomas had been upset, but after Quinn explained the grief that Leah was working through, he understood her actions.

At the end of the evening, Thomas was surrounded by his Irish relatives and felt doubly blessed. It was strange to be a part of two different families in two totally different parts of the world. Still, he had been embraced by this wonderful group, and he didn't feel like he was betraying the family that he spent the first 28 years of his life with.

The following morning he woke with a banger of a headache. How did they convince him last night, while drinking pints, to have a business meeting first thing in the morning with Quinn and his brother Brody? He was totally unprepared and very hungover. He needed to drink at least a pot of coffee before he left. He met them in the kitchen, and the three of them drove to the office. He was shocked at the high-tech offices and realized that the building also had a lab and testing facility. He was taken into the meeting room, where both Colleen and Regan were already seated. They said hello, and Colleen pushed a button that sent a projection screen down from the ceiling. When had they put this presentation together? He'd need to be careful when drinking Jameson with them in the future.

Colleen began, "McMillon Farms is the number one supplier of barley for the largest manufacturer of stout beer in Ireland." Quinn leaned over and winked at him as Colleen continued. "Barley is temperamental and doesn't produce a good yield if conditions aren't perfect. Some farms can only supply one out of every two to three years, but since we have farms in both the east and west of Ireland, we can provide a consistent amount of barley every year. We sometimes lose over one-third of our crops to weather, mainly rain. Regan attended Wageningen University & Research in the Netherlands which recently developed a type of barley that will grow in wet conditions. If we succeed, this could change the production of barley in all of Ireland. We would have the patent on a seed that every Irish farmer, or really farmers around the world, would want. It would bring jobs and help our economy.

There is a large farm down the road that has just become available. The owner is known to be fair, and if you work out an agreement with them to your liking, we would like to cultivate this brand new crop on the property. We would supply everything, but you would oversee it. We are a family-run business, and we would like to bring you in to run this new endeavor."

Colleen took a deep breath and sat down as Thomas looked from person to person at the table. He had been in Ireland for less than 48 hours, became part of a family, and was now offered a job? And a dream job at that. "Wow, I am floored by this offer and so honored that you have the confidence in me to spearhead this."

Brody interrupted, "I have to tell you, I was against a rash decision to hire Quinn's son, but I did some digging and researched you yesterday. You have definitely made your mark in agriculture. It would be an honor to have you at McMillon Farms."

"Come off, Uncle Brody," said Regan as she looked right into Thomas' eyes. "Irish blood needs no research, Thomas. Your veins run deep of McMillon. We would be vera blessed to work with our brother."

Quinn leaned over and winked at him again. "Can you let us know by Monday?"

"Absolutely," he said with excitement.

The day he had left to come to Ireland, Clare had asked him what he was hoping to find. He had simply said, "Peace."

"Go and find your peace," she said. "My only tie to Savannah is you, and my home is wherever you are. We are together in this. I know that you will always make the best decisions for our family."

He thought about that conversation while he was in the Shrine's adoration chapel. Could he and Clare make their lives here? Could they have children and raise them in Ireland? All the pieces seem to be coming to him as he prayed for answers. He knew the last part of the puzzle was to see the new farm, so Quinn drove him out to the property on Saturday.

It was a few miles away from McMillon Farms, just past a dairy farm. The road was long and narrow, with an Irish stone fence running down each side. The two-story house was located right over the brick fence, close to the street, with a stream running down its side. It had an herb garden that had been well attended to and three goats in the meadow. It was something right off the pages of a picture book.

He walked the property and dug his hand into the dirt, rubbed it between his fingers, and put it to his nose. It was good fertile land. He jumped on top of the stone fence, looked around, closed his eyes, and found it: peace!

"I think I'd like to meet with the owner," Thomas said.

"The owner hasn't been to Ireland in over 25 years," Quinn answered.

"How can I reach them?" he inquired further.

"Just call home. This land belongs to your mum."

# LAND OF KENNY

As soon as Kathleen and Jack's plane landed, they went straight to the farm. Harry, the taxi driver, dropped them off in the driveway, and they began walking along the path, past the long stone fence. They could see the herb garden in the distance and the blur of a man who was digging in the soil. Kathleen froze. "Jack," she said in a whisper. "It's from my dream." Everything she was holding tumbled to the ground, and she broke into a run. As she got closer and closer, the figure began to come into focus. He must have sensed her presence because as he looked up, a huge grin spread across Thomas' face. The face that she loved since the second he was born.

She almost knocked him over when she finally reached him, and he burst out laughing. He had no idea of why his mom was sobbing as they stood in the garden swaying back and forth in a huge hug. But she knew. All of the pieces fell into place. Jack caught up with her and watched the scene unfold. She had talked about it so many times over the past few weeks. He wrapped his arms around the two of them, both out of love and protection, and realized that Thomas was exactly where he was meant to be....Ireland.

Kathleen pulled back from the group, reached inside her shirt and pulled off the Celtic Cross necklace. She let it ravel into her hand. Looking down at it, she gave it a quick kiss. She placed it into Thomas' hand and closed his fingers over it for safe keeping. "This is our family's Celtic Cross. It belongs to the heir of the estate, and that is now you. It is your duty to take over this land, and to have an heir that will do the same. Promise me."

Thomas gave her a sideways glance and started to snicker, so she asked him more sternly, "Promise me?"

He burst out laughing, "Okay, Okay Mom. You sound so serious. I promise." He looked down at the cross and placed it around his neck. "I'm the heir, huh? Well, can the HEIR put in a request for some of your Parmesan Chicken for dinner tonight?"

She swatted his arm, "Don't press your luck, boy."

As they teased one another, something beside the house caught Kathleen's eye. The Pink Lady. She disappeared into the back doorway of Brian's hermit cottage while Kathleen followed quickly behind. When she entered into the room, the orb of the pink lady drifted over an old photograph beside Brian's bed. Kathleen had never noticed it before. The old family photo showed a family of three, and she recognized two of them. The father stood in the back wearing a top hat, a young Brian stood beside him, and sitting in front of them both was the mom, the Pink Lady.

Kathleen followed the bright sphere with her eyes. "You were checking on me, weren't you? You followed the Celtic Cross necklace and were watching the heir of this land. Well, you will be happy to know that it is now home...both the necklace and the heir."

The bright ball of the pink lady floated to the center of the room and ever so slowly shrunk until nothing remained. Kathleen looked to the doorway where Jack and Thomas were staring at her, befuddled.

"Did you boys see that?" she asked. But judging from the looks on their faces, she knew the answer. They both nodded their heads quickly, waiting for an explanation. Kathleen grinned sheepishly and continued, "How much do you guys know about Fairies?"

~

Colin Thomas Murray was baptized at the Shrine of Our Lady of Knock on October 3. Father Dillon performed the ceremony, and a choir, made up of Clare's school pupils, sang like angels. They already loved Clare even though she had only been teaching them for a short while. After the baptism, everyone was invited to Thomas and Clare's home to celebrate. With all of the family present, the house was packed. As usual, his Savannah family was in rare form and were the life of the party, while his Irish family simply grinned with enjoyment.

Kathleen and Anne had stolen away a few moments down by the stream. They had found two cut-off logs sitting face up and had used them for seats as they listened to the flowing stream moving over the rocks. Anne leaned over and placed a wildflower in Kathleen's lap saying, "I can't believe you got me into the House of Brigid, Mom. I absolutely love Dublin."

Anne had been upset with her mother, and Kathleen

knew she must make it right. Kathleen had replayed their argument over and over in her mind. She regretted her parenting mistake. One night, as she and Jack were sitting in adoration, she read a University of Notre Dame pamphlet that someone had left in the pew. The University had started a community in two different places in Ireland. The House of Brigid, in Dublin, invited recent college graduates to immerse themselves in Irish culture and Celtic spirituality. Kathleen had blurted out, "Oh my gosh, Jack. Anne's right!" He had shushed her and asked if they could talk later, but she left him sitting alone and ran out the Chapel door. This opportunity had Anne's name all over it.

Anne had squealed when Kathleen started explaining the program, knowing she might begin the following September. After what seemed like a long and painful wait, she got word that she had been accepted. She was giving Anne the chance that Kathleen didn't get before she was engaged: the opportunity to live independently and to travel.

She picked up the flower from her lap and smiled at Anne. "Your happiness shows on your face. I knew you would love Ireland. Plus, Thomas is lucky to have his kid sister living just a short trip away."

As they walked back towards the house, Kathleen asked Anne to go ahead while she quickly stopped at the cemetery beyond the house. She had been there before to find her ancestors, and now she was back to bid goodbye to Brian. She pulled out an old piece of glass that she had picked up beside the Hawthorn and placed it on his gravestone. "The light always hit these pieces of glass just right, didn't they, Brian? They made me think I saw lights in the field," she said into the breeze. As she looked at the new gravestone sitting among the old, Quinn walked up. They hadn't been alone since she arrived, and she was happy to have a moment to talk.

"How did you know that Brian had passed?" he asked.

"Brian told me, before I left Ireland, that I had second sight just like many of my Kenny ancestors. I didn't believe him at the time and still don't completely understand it, but he was right. He came and told me goodbye the night of his passing," she answered. A burst of wind hit her in the face and blew her hair into her eyes.

Quinn watched her intently. "You haven't changed one bit over the years. You still have the spunk of a 25-year-old but now have a band of fairies at your bidding."

She wagged her finger at him and said, "Yeah, you better not get on my bad side," and let out a giggle.

He laughed and raised his hands like he was innocent. Then he looked around the land and said, "I can't believe Brian left you all of this. He really loved you. He knew that you would take care of the Kenny land."

"Should we be worried about Gray?" she asked.

Quinn explained, "The Garda are looking for him. They questioned him after mum found Brian, and they instructed Gray to stay in Knock if they needed to ask him anything further. There were serious questions around Brian's death, and when the Garda came back, he was gone. Sean said he had come into Dowling's acting crazy. He said that Gray was ranting and raving about the farm being haunted. He claimed that something kept locking him out of the house, hiding his keys, and that dirt was always on the bristles of his toothbrush. Either he went crazy, or Brian got the last laugh. He knows the police want him for questioning for attempted murder. Don't worry, he won't be back."

Kathleen nodded slowly, processing what Quinn had said

before asking him about another worry. "What about Leah? Thomas said she made quite a scene at the party you threw for him."

"Leah will be fine. She misses Maura and doesn't have anyone else. Her parents are both gone, and she runs that store by herself. She spent her whole life watching out for her wee sister and never took the time to have a life of her own. She's grieving, just like we all are."

Kathleen smiled and patted his arm, remembering how sweet Maura had been to her and sympathizing over his last year without his wife. Then, looking around, she blurted out. "This place isn't the same without Brian."

Quinn focused on the herb garden, "It's not, but yet it still is. Can't you still feel him?" Kathleen smiled and nodded as Quinn continued, "Wouldn't he be happy to know a true Kenny descendant is farming this land once again?" He narrowed his gaze at Kathleen and slightly shook his head. "Ya know, I was shocked when I came upon Thomas in your family photo. I was so angry and hurt, wondering how you could have deprived me of 28 years with my son. It was Jack that gave me another point of view, but Dillon was the one who put it in perspective, that it was God's timing. Thomas is a part of my life now, and I am most grateful for that."

Kathleen sighed, "I'm so sorry, Quinn. When we found out, Thomas was five years old, and we had two younger children. I was trying to protect my family. I realize now that in protecting them, I was hurting you. I'm so very sorry. Can you forgive me?"

Quinn looked her in the eyes and nodded, then he turned to look out to the field. "I was happy when you called to tell me that Thomas was on his way to Ireland to find me, but even happier at the thought that he might want to stay. Your offer to give him this land to farm was an amazing opportunity for both Thomas and all of the McMillon's. We were looking for land to plant the new crop, and someone with experience to handle it. This land is very fertile, and Thomas is the perfect person to oversee it. He will do well here, and we are so blessed to have him."

Kathleen told him that Thomas had been shocked that she owned the land. "Jack and I were working with Brian's lawyer, trying to finalize my taking ownership of the property. After signing the final papers, I could deed the land to Thomas, but I had a couple of stipulations. I tried to explain why he can't take down that lone hawthorn tree." She smiled sheepishly at Quinn. She still didn't believe in fairies, but Brian had been right about so many other things, she might have to open her eyes to the possibility. "I also asked Thomas to please keep Brian's room as-is. This grandma is planning lots of visits. Jack and I will be staying for a couple of more weeks, so there will be plenty of time to work out all the details. A lot has hit Thomas at once: finding out about you, moving to Ireland for his dream job, having a baby, and owning a farm, all in a couple of months. But he is truly happy.

Quinn asked her if she were sure she wanted to give up the land. "It belongs to you, you know," Quinn said.

Kathleen's eyes began welling with tears, "It belongs to the Kenny heir, our son: mine, Jack's, and yours."

She had come full circle from tracing her past, finding her future with Jack, and embracing the past again for her Irish son. She wished she could have hugged Brian one last time, but she knew now that it wasn't God's path for her to live in Ireland; it was her son's.

When Quinn saw Jack coming down the path, he turned

to leave Kathleen alone in her thoughts. As the two men passed each other, Thomas' dad and his father, they nodded in mutual respect. Jack walked up behind Kathleen, smiled, and wrapped his arms around her. All of a sudden, there it was.

All of her senses were alive, and she felt a stirring deep in her soul. She did a quick scan of her surroundings, appreciating how God put all of the pieces together in His own time. She settled into his hug and was happy to feel the embrace of her home: Jack.

THE END

## ALSO IN THE SAINTS OF SAVANNAH SERIES

### THE SAVANNAH GONDOLIER

***From the characters that you loved from THE BLESSING OF THE CELTIC CURSE, comes the story of Maggie and Leo.***

***Her company was the prize in a late-night poker game.***

Maggie didn't need her Marketing degree to drive a trolley around Savannah for the past 14 years. When her father wins a run-down kayaking company in a poker game, she trades in her trolley uniform for a paddle and jumps at the opportunity to get paid for doing something she loves: kayaking.

***He is a gondolier escaping from shame in Venice.***

Leo once thought that being a gondolier was everything he ever wanted, but that all changed after his father's accident and the circumstances surrounding it. When Leo decides to leave Venice, he is drawn to where his family spent their carefree summers: Tybee Island.

***Will the water that brings them together divide them in the end?***

Maggie must find a way to help Leo without losing what she loves. Beautiful places and lovable characters make this novel a stay-with-you-forever read.

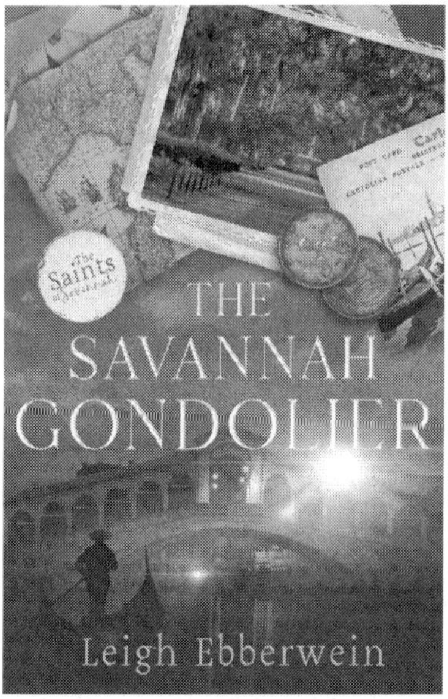

## LOOKING FOR SOMETHING FUN TO DO IN SAVANNAH?

**Look no further...**

**SAINTS OF SAVANNAH BAR CRAWL** - Follow a fun route to the tribes favorite bars. Learn fun facts about Savannah while sipping the best drinks in town. You might see a ghost, or two, along the way.

WARNING: Savannah has an Open Container Policy - We don't call this a crawl for nothing!

**KATHLEEN AND JACK'S DATE NIGHT** - Follow a night full of excellent food and drinks intertwined with lots of romance.

WARNING - Hand holding REQUIRED!

For more information, subscribe to Leighebberwein.com.

ACKNOWLEDGEMENT

I couldn't have written this book without the love and support of my husband, John. He encourages me to write, even amidst the chaos of our large family, and has patiently read over this book so many times that he probably knows it by heart. Our life together is the best adventure I could ever imagine.

I also would like to thank my children for being the best fan club any Mom could ever have. They read over my shoulder as I type and are very vocal about suggestions. Thank you to my parents for always loving what I write and my sister for talking through scenes to make them more realistic.

Thank you to my college roommates who traveled to Ireland with me for "research." We trudged through snow, sleet and a bomb cyclone....yes, that is a thing. We never stopped laughing and I look forward to many more trips. You are my tribe.

A huge thanks go out to my writing critique partner and

friend, Meggie Daly, and my Advance Reader Team. Your encouragement and support have kept me going.

Last, but certainly not least, I'd like to thank Monsignor James Costigan, a sweet Irish priest who was preaching the 7:30 a.m. daily Mass on July 12, 2019. My husband, John, and I had left the children at home sleeping on that hot summer morning, and snuck off to Mass together. The readings of the day were Gen 46:1-7, 28-30, the story of Jacob and Joseph. Just like many Irish storytellers, Monsignor told the tale of an Irish boy who went in search of his father. Needless to say, my mind wandered in church that day....but please don't tell that to the good Monsignor.

For more information on Our Lady of Knock, visit
https://www.knockshrine.ie

# HEMOCHROMATOSIS - THE CELTIC CURSE

Although my novel is fiction, Hemochromatosis is NOT. My family has been directly affected by this genetic disorder. Thankfully, my father-in-law informed us of the disease that he was fighting. Through his compassionate nudging, we respectfully tested our children early and were able to treat them promptly.

Iron is an essential nutrient found in many foods. Iron carries oxygen (in hemoglobin) to all parts of the body. Typically, humans absorb about 8-10% of the iron in foods that they eat. People with hemochromatosis (too much iron) can absorb four times more iron than average.

Over time, these excesses build up in major organs such as the heart, liver, pancreas, joints, and pituitary. If the extra iron is not removed, these organs can become diseased. Untreated hemochromatosis can be fatal.

Most commonly, the treatment is simple blood donations to get iron levels down to normal. However, these levels need to be monitored over time.

Genetic tests can help identify family members who are at risk for hemochromatosis. The genetic test is usually performed with a cheek swab. These tests are also included with services like Ancestry DNA. Confirmation must be obtained by Iron panel test.

In loving memory of Joseph Keeshen Ebberwein
1935 - 2021
*May God hold you in the palm of his hand*

For more information:

Hemochromatosis.org

*Information was gathered from Hemochromatosis.org which is a digital education and awareness effort provided by Iron Disorders Institute. https://www.hemochromatosis.org/*

# ABOUT THE AUTHOR

*Leigh Ebberwein was raised under the watchful eyes of Savannah's steadfast and caring community. After graduating from the all-girls Catholic high school, she graduated from Georgia Southern University in Business. For the next 25 years, she was the VP for a fast and growing company...her family of nine.*

*In 2019, Leigh picked up a pen and began writing in a marble black composition book that belonged to one of her children. Although always a storyteller, only at that moment did Leigh realize her call to write down her stories.*

*Leigh and her husband live near a creek on the outskirts of Savannah. Warm breezes, breathtaking sunsets, and a slew of children keep life rolling quicker than the outgoing tide. If not in the laundry room, Leigh may be found in her garden or on the back porch scribbling away with a cup of coffee nearby.*

*Savannah whispers its quirky, unique stories to Leigh. Her loveable characters have already found a welcoming fan base in Savannah's fiction lovers. Leigh thanks you for giving her the privilege of entertaining you—if only for a little while!*

If you love the beauty of Savannah, the shenanigans of the Irish, or the comfort of a good book in your hand...stop in for a visit to Leighebberwein.com. You'll find questions for your Book Club, live video scenes, up to date information on future books and so much more.

Made in the USA
Columbia, SC
12 September 2022

66880025R00143